On Sunset

ALSO BY KATHRYN HARRISON

Nonfiction

The Kiss: A Memoir
Seeking Rapture: Scenes from a Woman's Life
The Road to Santiago
Saint Thérèse of Lisieux
The Mother Knot: A Memoir
While They Slept: An Inquiry into the Murder of a Family
Joan of Arc: A Life Transfigured
True Crimes: A Family Album

Fiction

Thicker Than Water
Exposure
Poison
The Binding Chair
The Seal Wife
Envy
Enchantments

On Sunset

A MEMOIR

Kathryn Harrison

Doubleday *New York*

www.doubleday.com

DOUBLEDAY and the portrayal of an anchor with a dolphin are registered trademarks of Penguin Random House LLC.

Book design by Maria Carella
Jacket design by John Fontana
Front-of-jacket photographs: portrait courtesy of the author; photo frames © azure1/Shutterstock; wallpaper © David Lichtneker/ Arcangel

Library of Congress Cataloging-in-Publication Data

Names: Harrison, Kathryn, author.
Title: On Sunset : a memoir / by Kathryn Harrison.
Description: First edition. | New York : Doubleday, [2018]
Identifiers: LCCN 2018019959| ISBN 9780385542678 (hardcover) | ISBN 9780385542685 (ebook)
Subjects: LCSH: Harrison, Kathryn—Childhood and youth. | Harrison, Kathryn—Family. | Novelists, American—20th century—Family relationships. | BISAC: BIOGRAPHY & AUTOBIOGRAPHY / Personal Memoirs. | BIOGRAPHY & AUTOBIOGRAPHY / Literary. | BIOGRAPHY & AUTOBIOGRAPHY / Rich & Famous.
Classification: LCC PS3558.A67136 Z46 2018 | DDC 818/.5403 [B]—dc23 LC record available at https://lccn.loc.gov/2018019959

MANUFACTURED IN THE UNITED STATES OF AMERICA

10 9 8 7 6 5 4 3 2 1

First Edition

FOR JULIA

For darkness
restores what light cannot repair.

—JOSEPH BRODSKY

On Sunset

IT'S HARD TO get me to fall asleep. It wouldn't be, if I weren't kept on a Victorian nursery schedule that delivers me to bed before the sun goes down. To object that no child goes to bed at seven o'clock, not in the fourth grade, would only bolster my grandmother's resolve to do whatever possible to shield me from the pernicious influence of American children. Never mind that we live in Los Angeles and that I was born in 1961; my childhood belongs to my mother's parents, who, in the way of old people, have returned themselves to their pasts, taking me along.

Because my grandfather's widowed mother had been destitute, she couldn't afford philosophies of child-rearing. Her attention was fixed on just feeding her four children, of whom my grandfather was the youngest. So it is my grandmother's early years, insulated by vast wealth and managed by nursemaids and governesses, that determine the course of first my mother's and then my own childhood.

There's no money to employ a governess, not anymore, but my grandmother is tyrant enough. I curtsy when introduced to adults. I endure mustard plasters, cod liver oil, and other torments generally imagined to be reserved for children left behind in a previous century. I am not allowed chewing gum, carbonated beverages, nail varnish, or to go to bed with damp hair. Peanut butter does not exist. I don't know what *Love, American Style* is, or why it in particular among television programs other children talk about has earned my grandmother's opprobrium. I'd trade Christmas and a birthday for permission to watch *The Brady Bunch,* episodes of which I've seen at other children's homes and recognized as a valuable resource, answering my curiosity about drive-in movies, blue jeans, and other contemporary American blunders, like Twinkies, that remain out of reach. In sunny Southern California, no day achieves a temperature that frees me from wearing a cotton vest under my school uniform blouse. If such things could be procured, I'd be forced to use a hook to button my shoes and a stick to chase my hula hoop.

As my grandmother is not one to negotiate, there is nothing to be done about bedtime, except to keep my grandfather beside me. If he tries to kiss me goodnight before I am asleep, I get up and follow him out of my room. It doesn't matter that I can unspool his life in my head, tell myself every story. All that matters is keeping him by my side.

"Say your father's name."

"You know my father's name."

"But I like to hear you say it."

"Emmanuel."

Uh man you el. I make the word silently, feeling how the *m* draws my lips to meet and briefly touch.

"Emmanuel means angel," I say.

"Emmanuel means 'God is with us.' He loved to run, my father did. Loved to try to outpace the coaches. Horse-drawn coaches, going from London to Brighton and places."

"Why did he?"

"For the fun of it, that's all."

"You didn't know your father."

"No. He died when I was nine months old. A very handsome man, they told me. Uncommonly tall for a man born in 1861. So my mother—"

"How tall?"

"Six feet, four inches."

My grandfather is tall too. Black-and-white photographs of him as a young man don't show his blue eyes. But he was handsome, his countenance untroubled by the hardships he'd endured, the thousands of penniless miles he'd traveled.

"Isn't an angel of God talking to you?" I ask. He sits by my bed with a hand cupped behind his better ear, as if to catch and funnel words into its dark canal.

"Is that what the Sunday school teacher says?"

"No." Christian Science doesn't have angels, only *Science and Health with Key to the Scriptures* and a chalky blue pencil for underlining the important parts.

"So my mother's parents loaned her what she needed to

Harry Samuel Jacobs, 1916, Alaska.

Margaret Esme Sassoon Benjamin, Shanghai, 1900.

rent a house," my grandfather continues before I can interrupt again, "and she took in what were called paying guests."

"Like a boardinghouse," I say.

"Like a boardinghouse," he agrees, as unashamed of having grown up poor as my grandmother is of having been raised in conspicuous luxury, safe inside the walls of privilege while outside a cart and horse moved through Shanghai's International Settlement collecting night soil from the coolies whose responsibility it was to empty their employers' chamber pots. As the Chinese used human waste to fertilize their crops, farmers prized the excrement of the rich and well-fed.

"You never knew your father." It seems to be a property of fathers in my family to misplace themselves. I have never known mine, and my fatherless grandfather is fully father to me.

"He died of consumption when I was nine months old."

"Galloping consumption," I say of the thing that overtook the great runner. I don't have to close my eyes to see everything disappear in the wake of a blood-drenched coach pulled by a blood-red Pegasus. No mortal can outpace it. Anyone on whom a drop falls sickens and dies.

"Tell me again who has wings on his sandals."

"Mercury. So my poor mother was penniless," he goes on, "with four little children, and in London that was tough skidding in those days."

London, 1891, without cars or electricity, without medicine that might have saved his father's life, when food was kept in an *icebox,* which is what I call our refrigerator, its thick black cord plugged into the wall. I call the stove a *cooker,* and because we have one of each, I allude to *washboards* and *mangles.* Flashlights are *torches,* margarine is *oleo,* and our cupboards are filled with names other children don't recognize: Peek Freans, Wilkin & Sons, McVitie's, Crosse & Blackwell, Huntley & Palmers, Marmite, Tate & Lyle, Colman's, Fortnum & Mason. As it says on lids and labels, all of them work for Her Majesty the Queen, by appointment. Apparently it was Queen Elizabeth who told Early's of Witney to make prickly wool blankets and Liberty of London to sell itchy wool scarves.

My speech is accessorized with words that never traveled as far west as the New World, like *swiz,* for swindle, and *elevenses,* a midmorning break for tea and biscuits. Whatever we have for dessert, even if it's pie à la mode, we call *pudding.* Away from home I know not to refer to checkers as *draughts,* pullovers as *jumpers,* French fries as *chips,* car trunks as *boots,* washcloths as *flannels,* or—especially—Dalmatian dogs as *spotted dicks.* I don't suffer the conceit that Hawaii remains *the Sandwich Islands,* refer to galoshes as *rubbers,* or call apartments *flats.* I don't end the alphabet with *zed.* But I make the occasional misstep. I ask a classmate to *be a brick* when I want to borrow her colored pencils, and call my allowance *pin money.* I never remember if it's *honor* or *honour,* apologize or *apologise.* When the time comes, I'll call

Margaret Esme Sassoon Benjamin, Shanghai, 1903.

feminine hygiene products *S.T.'s,* for *sanitary towels*—a girl's circumlocution, but of the wrong era. Language, like everything else, serves my grandmother's intent, pinning me to a time and place other than my own.

IT'S ALWAYS TWILIGHT in my London, because I don't like leaving out the man who lights the gas lamps, making his way through a pea-soup fog that spills over the cobbles and puddles around his shoes. He lifts his long wand to the top of each post and leaves a little flame behind. A bright string, like Christmas lights, follows him down the block. There are chimney pots and chimney sweeps. Hokey-pokey men scoop ice cream from their carts and serve it on squares of the previous day's newspaper.

"What flavor?" I want to know.

"Vanilla, it must have been."

"What else?"

"There was only the one."

My grandfather's grandfather, Samuel Jacobs, is there. He's a fishmonger who sells poultry too. "Executives used to come into his store to buy poultry or fish and take it home to their wives," my grandfather says.

As with the people who reside in his mother's boarding-house, the men who take fish to their wives are, my grandfather makes sure I understand, respectable businessmen. He doesn't tell me that gangs of ruffians, like the one his brother would join, plague the neighborhood where they live. But one day when he's hanging my coat in the hall closet, he dislodges a walking stick, and it falls to the floor at my feet.

"My father's," he says as he picks it up. He shows me

how the bottom unscrews from the top, revealing a gleaming long knife.

"Did he use it?" I watch my grandfather's hands screw the halves back into a single stick and tuck it behind the coats so that it disappears into the shadow it fell out of.

"I imagine he carried it as a precaution," he says, but he doesn't say against what, or whom.

My grandfather never speaks of squalor or want, so I never think to include them when I tell myself the stories he tells me. It will be decades before I am putting my own children to bed and am given occasion to consider tales I was told and what I might have failed to understand at the time. An oral history recorded toward the end of my grandfather's life offers enough clues to pass along to an archivist in London, who drills down into census reports from 1891, 1901, and 1911 and confirms my grandfather's report that his mother's paying guests were decent working people. The 1911 census lists her "visitors" as an antiques dealer, a seamstress, a bookstall manager and his son.

The family's own living quarters were cramped and poorly insulated. There was never enough heat, no more than there was food or rest. In 1891, the year Emmanuel Jacobs died, at twenty-nine, consumption galloped off with 134,000 Londoners. Measles, diphtheria, scarlet fever, whooping cough, typhoid, cholera: each took its share as well. Women labored at home, with or without a midwife, and some died in childbirth, or their babies died, or both of them did. My grandfather's brother, Sigmund, called "Sid," had a twin who died in infancy, but he doesn't speak of this ghost, any more than my grandmother does her dead brother. When he explains what chilblains are, he never says he knows because he's had them.

"Is a fishmonger's wife a person who screams about fish?" I ask, having heard the expression that suggests she is.

"She calls out to people in the market that she has fish for sale."

"So she does scream about fish."

"My grandfather had a store," he says, "not an outdoor market stall, so my grandmother would not have needed to scream like a fishwife if she worked in the shop, which she did not."

There's a station for the stagecoaches, and a blacksmith to shoe the horses that try to outrun my great-grandfather. Icemen sell ice, tinkers mend pots and pans, gentlemen wear top hats for no better reason than taking a walk outside. Smokestacks belch soot into the sky, staining everything, people too. Their faces get dirty just walking down the street and their clothes do too. Women's dresses drag along the streets and the heels of their shoes get caught between cobblestones. There's an asylum for my grandfather's sisters, Belle and Violet, meagerly schooled and fed by the Crown— day pupils among orphans, midday dinner included—while their mother pinched and squirreled and sacrificed all she could for my grandfather's and his brother's education. It wasn't an uncommon choice in London in the 1890s, nor held to be an unkind one; it doesn't strike me as any more peculiar than the rest of my grandfather's life, which took him so far north that half the year it's daytime and the other half it's night, a land so frozen that he traveled by dogsled, so cold that if you ran ten steps your lungs froze. I am not so concerned about his sisters as I am about his travails in boarding school, where his ears were boxed even more routinely than his backside was caned. Boxed until they rang inside.

I want to know what it means, ears that ring. Is it a church bell or is it a doorbell? Maybe it's the phone. I've stood in my room, fists aimed at either side of my head, and struck my own ears, but not very hard. Not hard enough to break my eardrums, or even hurt very much. Ten years after my grandfather left boarding school, when he was a young man working on the railroad—part of a team of surveyors for the Alaskan Engineering Commission, laying track all the way north to Fairbanks—the clamor amplified the ringing in his ears. Sometimes it's distant, others he can't help hearing the past, as its shrill cry drowns out the present.

"What if a bear was chasing you?"

"Then you were out of luck," he says.

"Why don't the bear's lungs freeze?"

"Because he's a polar bear."

"Say about the trees."

"Say what about the trees?"

My grandfather (to the left of the sign) with surveyors, a sled, and a dog team, 1916.

"You know, that they exploded."

"Well, that's what they did. They went off like pistols. In Talkeetna—it was sixty-two below, *sixty-two*—we heard them explode, burst open in the dark."

"Because of the sap," I say.

"Because of the sap," he agrees. He's explained how it expands when it freezes, how it's mostly water. "So cold, take off your glove, touch metal, and you can't get it off. Can't get your hand off unless you leave the skin behind."

I consider this. "Do fingerprints grow back?" I ask, trying not to see the skinned flesh pour handfuls of its own blood onto the white snow.

"No," he says.

"Say the rivers." Three great rivers converge in the town of Talkeetna. My grandfather recites their names in the same order every time.

"The Talkeetna, Susitna, and Chulitna."

Tal keet naa, Su seet naa, Chu leet naa. Sometimes when I'm jumping rope or playing hopscotch, the syllables come skipping into my head and I can't get them out.

OUR FINANCIAL COLLAPSE is schizophrenic. We are desperately poor, and I lack for nothing. I have a new bicycle, and when I outgrow it, I have another. The dresses I wear to Sunday school, with their satin sashes and hand-smocked bodices, come from a store on Rodeo Drive, where my grandmother perches on the arm of a gold-legged chair to supervise as I am professionally zipped, buttoned, and tied up in bows. Trim in her pink Chanel suit, either that or a red one, she's wearing, as she does every day, the string of pearls her father gave her when she turned seventeen.

The saleslady turns me around by my shoulders so my grandmother can examine the dress from every angle. She smells of Chanel N° 5, and Chanel has made her red lipstick as well. Every week, Robert at Robinson's salon rinses her hair black to cover the gray, curls and sets it into the shape it has assumed all my life. A toenail, varnished pink, peeps out from each open-toed black suede sling-back pump. She swings one leg back and forth; restless, always restless. Even when sitting and silent, my grandmother conveys the pent-up energy of a cat waiting to pounce. She has petite pretty legs and wears stockings that come one at a time, not like my pairs of tights.

"Ridiculous to attach them," she says when I ask if the garter belt doesn't annoy her. "If you get a ladder in one leg, you have to throw away both."

Her hands are hot and smooth and softer than any I know, and her complexion olive, not as dark as her father's nor as white as the poet Siegfried Sassoon's or Sir Philip Sassoon's, both of whose fathers' brown Baghdadi skin was successfully whitewashed by milky Ashkenazi mothers selected from among the marriageable Rothschilds.

Because that's what my grandmother is: *a Sassoon.* It is one of the first things I know about her, as if being a Sassoon were like being a pianist or barrister: a vocation. Unlike my grandfather, photographs of whom show him at work, my grandmother does nothing before the camera. Doing nothing, she exists for the lens, and the lens for her. It's the same with words. All her life the name precedes and introduces

Foreign Investment Trend Turns to Southland Property

Evidencing further the trend of foreign-capital investment in Southern California property, a real estate transfer consummated in the week just ended revealed that a member of the well-known Sassoon banking family of Great Britain has purchased a new home in the western section of Los Angeles, with plans completed for permanent residence here.

The buyer, Miss Margaret. Esme Sassoon Benjamin, a relative of Sir Philip Sassoon, prominent British financier, arrived in Los Angeles recently following the closing of her town house in Chelsea, London suburb. Her father, the late S. Sassoon Benjamin, among other business interests, operated a large banking institution in Shanghai, China.

The property, just acquired for approximately $25,000, is situated at 360 Hilgard Ave., Westwood Hills, opposite the U.C.L.A. campus. It consists of a two-story four-bedroom Georgian-type residence with beautifully landscaped gardens, and was formerly owned by Mr. and Mrs. Richard A. Thorpe. Thorpe, well-known picture director, entered into negotiations for the sale a few weeks ago when he believed his transfer to London by the company by which he is employed would be permanent, but with the outbreak of the war he was recalled to Hollywood, arriving on the day the title to the property passed to the English buyer, it was disclosed.

The Guy Price Co., Beverly Hills realtors, conducted the negotiations in co-operation with Miss Gertrude Steinberg, acting for the Thorpes, and Arthur W. Isaacs representing Miss Benjamin.

her. In 1939, when she moves from Old World to New, her purchase of a home occasions an article in the *Los Angeles Times*.

She keeps the cutting among her expired passports, her parents' death certificates, and her immigration papers, as though such a thing could establish her identity as well as any of the official documents in the black enameled lockbox bearing her mother's initials. D.S.B. Dollie Sassoon Benjamin, the letters gilded. It did present my grandmother as a relative of Sir Philip, the kind of vulgar announcement she'd never make about herself but must have enjoyed seeing in the paper—the equivalent of a coming-out party, without the bother of the party itself. At forty, my grandmother was too old to be an ingénue, if she had ever been such a thing.

With respect to romance, the name Sassoon had caused her nothing but trouble, and at forty-two she married a man to whom it meant little, if it meant anything at all. Had my grandfather not happened to have married a Sassoon, he'd be unlikely ever to have heard of them. He never says what I hear other people say, that the Sassoons are the Rothschilds of the East. Instead he calls my grandmother's family a "very wealthy clan from Persia," managing to exalt and dismiss them at once.

"OH, YOU SHOULD have seen them!" my grandmother says of the shoes she wore as a young woman. "They came in the door before we did!" If I ever wear such shoes, she assures me, my toes will be irreparably pinched  and squashed and I'll never be able to wear Mary Janes again. She watches the salesman use his thumb to press my big toe down on the metal device he uses to measure feet, as if to force it into a more honest accounting of itself.

Black patent leather, so shiny that when I lean over to buckle them I see my face looking back at me out of the mirror of each toe, Mary Janes are the antidote to the misery of Sunday school dresses, which demand white tights and the further restriction of white gloves that come home gray, as I can pay strict attention to my fingers and what they might encounter for only so long. Were it possible to undo the tiny slippery buttons on the wrist of one hand with the gloved fingers of the other, I'd strip them off as soon as I was out of sight, the way I do barrettes and hairbands, but these gloves have been made to thwart the wearer's attempts to remove them.

"Why is it called patent?" I ask as I watch my grandfather open the lid of the box, part the tissue paper, and take the new shoes out from between the white folds. He uses the big scissors from his desk, opened wide, to score their slick leather soles with the tip of one blade. First he goes one way, then the other, crisscross.

"Because the process of making leather hard and shiny was patented."

"Who was he?" I ask after my grandfather explains what a patent is, but he doesn't know the inventor's name.

"Now I won't slip," I say when he hands me the shoes.

"Now you won't slip," he agrees.

The first few times I wear a new pair outside, I carry them from the house to the car so their soles won't touch the ground. But it's of little use; I'm delaying the inevitable, as I can't run in my tights from car door to church door. I slip into the red plastic Sunday school chair and before I open my *Key to the Scriptures* I examine the sole of one shoe to consider its complexion. Even if I'm careful where I tread, choosing grass over concrete where I can, already it will bear pockmarks. In a month or two, the lines my grandfather scored into the leather will have disappeared.

Other families have sheets, whereas we sleep on bed-clothes made to order from La Grande Maison de Blanc, hand-finished and monogrammed. Once a week they are pulled rumpled from the mattresses, left in a bundle on the service steps by the kitchen, and returned washed, folded, ironed, and wrapped in blue paper tied with white string. Twice a week our housekeeper, Tina, leaves bottles outside the kitchen door for the milkman, who comes and goes in the night, exchanging empty for full. Sometimes, as I am awake as early as I am put to bed, I hear the milkman's square truck laboring up our long driveway. The soles of his shoes are silent, but the glass bottles rattle in their wire carrier as he walks toward the house.

Milk, eggs, racks of recharged soda bottles, dry clean-
ing: all of these are delivered. Whereas other families pay
bills, we are *dunned* for such extravagances, harbingering our
arrival at *debtors' prison.*

It doesn't take a grownup to understand that the rem-
edies for our predicament are quaint. My grandmother collects Blue Chip trading stamps. The more she spends at the
market, the more roll out from the blue machine next to
the cash register. At home, as soon as the groceries are put
away, she puts the stamps away too, in a shoebox she keeps
in a drawer in the mahogany sideboard I am not allowed to
touch, as it is being preserved by the notion that its value,
yet to be established, will reshingle the roof, replaster the
inside of the pool, and resurface the driveway too—that
it has the power to smooth things out in general. Once a
month, on a Saturday afternoon, after ballet, which I am to
learn (like it or not, and I don't) as a corrective to climbing
trees (this is my mother's idea), my grandmother and I sit
together in the breakfast nook and paste them into flimsy
orange booklets made for that purpose.

"Catch that, will you, darling?" she says when a stamp
or two falls from her side of the table, and I scoot forward
and slide down the cracked red vinyl of the banquette seat
until I am squatting before her feet, around which I always
find others, which have floated down undetected.

"What is debtors' prison?" I ask from under the table.

"It's where you end up when you haven't paid your bills."
She folds sheets of the big Super 10 stamps along their perforations to create five-by-ten stamp blocks that she whisks
over the wet sponge set in the saucer between us and slaps

onto the pages crookedly, going too fast to be tidy, ignoring the grids of dotted lines.

Because I have nimble fingers, I do the little stamps, the ones like pocket change, pennies no one bothers to pick up. Slow and meticulous, I wet the single ones gently and fit them carefully into the grid printed for that purpose, gumming each on just so, trying to align all the halved circles of the broken perforations so they look as if they were never torn apart from one another, my page of little stamps as seamless as her pages of big ones.

"Will we wear uniforms?"

My grandmother looks up as I resurface. "I suppose we will have to wait and see," she says.

"What about my mother?" It seems only fair that she should have to come too, as I know from fights I can't help but overhear that she spends every dime we have on shoes. She is disrespectful, irresponsible, beastly, selfish, promiscuous, and sharper than snakes' teeth. And how it is that she doesn't realize her roommate is a lesbian, and, what's worse, in love with her, is a mystery of such proportion that it can stand among the seven wonders of the earth.

If my mother lived at home with us, she'd be less expensive—and removed from the company of her allegedly amorous roommate—but no one has ever suggested she move back in. Even I, who grieved at her leaving, was relieved once she'd left.

She visits only when she's ready, tearing up the driveway unannounced, spoiling for a fight about money or men or whether or not lesbianism is communicable, but no one wins a fight with my grandmother. Her tactics are unscrupulous. Also, she has what my mother calls an *idée fixe* inspired by her sister Cecily's notorious domestic arrangements, a public (if confined to France) outrage that includes—as it has all of my great-aunt's adult life—not one but two lovers at the same time. Or, as my grandmother calls them, spongers.

According to my mother, my grandmother suffers a great number of *idées fixes*, thereby making her my mother's *bête noir.*

"Oh, for fuck's sake, Mother," she says. She never wastes an opportunity to use the *f*-word. She's so young we're mistaken for sisters.

And not just by strangers. My grandparents receive me as an unexpected late-life child, an obedient younger sister to balance out the misdeeds of the older one. No one admits I've inherited the kind of fairy-tale task impossible

Miss Smeaton, Miss Herrer, and Cecily, to the far right, capering for my grandmother's camera, Japan, 1917.

to accomplish without magic. I am both my mother's worst mistake come to life, and the one expected to redeem what's too late to undo: In utero, I permanently defaced her teenage body. I drew spiteful silver stretch marks from her hips to her navel, and I painted spidery blue veins on the backs of her thighs. When I arrived, incarnate and demanding, the sight and sound of me inspired a postpartum collapse from which my mother never rebounded.

"A bracelet is a fucking bracelet, it isn't a declaration of undying love." The object under consideration hangs insolently from my mother's wrist, a circle of linked sterling disks, each enameled with a tiny Viking scene, black boats on blue waves with an orange pinprick of a midnight sun that never sets. She pinches it tighter to show me it needs two disks removed and says I can have the ones the jeweler takes out. Ever since her roommate, Ingrid, brought it back from Norway, the gift has remained on my mother's arm, provoking countless arguments, each of which further cements her commitment to leave the offending object where it is, because the most effective means of punishing my grandmother is to suggest that her fears are grounded in truth: my mother is a lesbian and the bracelet as good as a betrothal.

"What about her?" my grandmother says, ostensibly returning to the topic of my spendthrift mother, but before I can answer she reminds me that bath time is approaching, it is time to finish with the stamps. My mother is a closed subject.

I count the booklets whose pages we've filled, as I do each time we pack up the stamps. It takes a great many of them—forty—each decorated by a repellent caricature of a grinning-so-wide-it's-a-grimace blue chipmunk, to purchase the toaster she's chosen from a little catalog of housewares and appliances. For some time now we have been stuck in the doldrums of the middle thirties. I never think how odd it must be for a woman who once traveled with a tower of Louis Vuitton steamer trunks (one holding a cage made of silk grosgrain ribbons woven around a frame that fit inside, to hold hats without crushing a feather or creasing a veil) to collect savings stamps for a toaster. I might if she complained, but she likes it, I can tell. The two of us are happily absorbed in the thriftiness of our occupation, serving the conceit of making a significant contribution to the family coffers.

HE PRUNES HIS fruit trees in a dress suit and tie, a white shirt he won't get dirty when digging in the garden, cufflinks he doesn't lose sieving leaves off the surface of the swimming pool. When it's hot, he hangs his jacket carefully on a fencepost, takes off his tie, folds it, and slips it in the jacket's pocket. He never buys new clothes. Those he has come out of sample cases, decades old, from when he was a traveling salesman. He buys underclothes, of course, and socks, and on Father's Day I go out with my grandmother to buy him pajamas or aftershave.

No matter what he does, I dog his heels with a bow he's made from a springy cut branch and a piece of twine. "Let me," I ask, reaching for his pocketknife, as I do every time, "Please?" But he keeps it out of reach while notching the ends of the branch.

"If you touched a frozen pole, would it pull off your calluses?" There's a long ridge of thick hard skin where his palm meets his four fingers, and small ones on the underside of

This boulder, nearly perfectly round, was dug from the foundation of our house. My grandfather used it in the landscaping.

each finger and thumb: gardening calluses, all of them, from using a spade or a hoe or the rake. The garden is big—a half acre—with orange, lemon, and lime trees, a fishpond with a waterfall, a vegetable garden, and too many flowers to count.

"Probably." He makes arrows too, using the blade to shave one end of a stick down to a dull point and notch the other so it doesn't slip off the twine when I pull it back and take aim. They don't fly straight or far, and the bow rarely lasts more than an afternoon. But there will be another the next day.

"I'm part Apache," I remind him.

"Are you?" We've had this conversation before.

"Or maybe Comanche, since he's from west Texas." My father is, according to my mother, one-eighth American Indian. He's also a preacher with a wife and another daughter. That's all I know about him.

My grandfather, to the far left, with members of the Talkeetna, June 1917.

"Why didn't the Indians you knew have bows and arrows?"

"Because the Indians I knew used traps." The Talkeetna competed with him for pelts, he tells me, because the Russians shanghaied them into slave labor.

"What do you mean, shanghaied?"

"Ship captains had a hard time getting crews to go to China," he says, explaining how the port city's name turned into a verb, "so they kidnapped them."

"Why didn't they want to go?" I ask, crawling around tree trunks, looking for lost arrows. He doesn't answer. They must have been afraid of cholera or typhus, or the rabid dogs.

Hydrophobia, as my grandmother calls the disease, remains a great concern of hers, and she explains with excited horror the treatment for having been bitten by an animal with rabies—needles plunged from the front to the back of you—and how her cousin Aziza was bitten on the knee and had to sit still in a chair for six months.

AMONG MY GRANDMOTHER'S papers is a Sassoon family tree, vast and nearly unreadable for want of pruning. The eight sons of Sheik Sassoon—David was the eldest living, my grandmother's great-grandfather Benjamin second in line—

Sassoons and Hayims of Baghdad.

produced something closer to an ancient sprawling banyan than a tidy oak with a single trunk: twenty-eight children and ninety-three grandchildren, my grandmother's father one of those ninety-three. Each branch bears first names that repeat throughout the tree, some as many as a dozen times—David, Benjamin, Aziza, Rebecca, Habiba, Hanini, Elis, Elias, Ezra, Mozelle, Hannah, Reuben, Joseph, Abraham, Ezekiel. Sometimes a Sassoon marries a Flora, Luna, or Regina; a Percival precedes the illustrious poet Siegfried; but they aren't any help in tracing first and second cousins who remove themselves willy-nilly one or more times, stymieing my attempts to find even my grandmother, though she's pointed herself out often enough. As there's only the one copy, which cannot be besmirched, my grandmother has said no, we cannot mark certain names, not even her own.

"If we use my blue Sunday school pencil, it will wipe off like chalk, the way it does from *Key to the Scriptures*."

"No," my grandmother says, "it will not wipe off, as you are not going to draw it on."

So I can never be certain which Hanini is my grandmother's Aunt Hanini or which Aziza is my grandmother's cousin Aziza. It makes no difference if our Ezekiel has a sister named Mozelle, not when another does as well, and the longer I look, the more likely it is that all the names, rendered in a foreign-looking cursive, will start to swarm over the paper. The family cannot be accommodated by two dimensions. There are too many Sassoons to flatten onto the page. But one day Aunt Aziza comes to tea and from memory draws the two branches that demonstrate her relationship to my grandmother and theirs to Sheik Sassoon. She tells me it's true she did have to sit in a chair for six months, and that no version of the family tree is accurate.

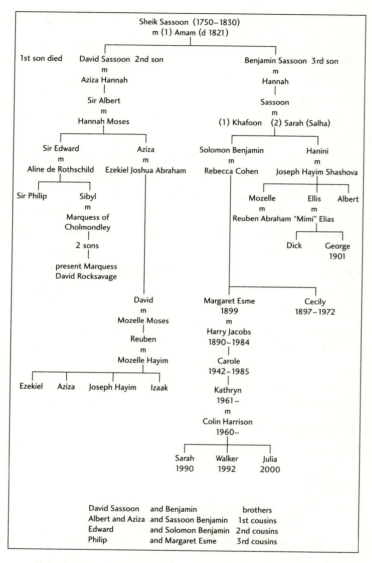

A fragment of the Sassoon family tree, demonstrating the connection between my grandmother and Sheik David, compiled from the archives of Naim Dangoor.

My great-grandfather, Solomon Sassoon Benjamin, is near the center, just below his half-sister, Khatoun, her name followed by the parenthetical aside, "Her mother died giving birth to her." It is the only such remark; others clarify titles and aristocratic connections. Two branches above my great-grandfather's immediate family, a different Solomon Benjamin Sassoon (on whose account my great-grandfather reversed the order of his own name, to avoid being mistaken in business dealings) is linked to a different Khatoun, by marriage rather than blood.

For now, all I know is, once upon a time, during the reign of the Ottoman Empire, a family of merchant princes arose. Under the city of Baghdad, the Sassoons stuffed their secret cellars with silks, spices, and pearls. Upstairs, their sons came of age in the countinghouse, an apprenticeship that delivered them to riches of their own. For David, afflicted, like my grandfather, with wanderlust, it carried him—wearing, it is fabled, a cloak lined with pearls—as far as Bombay, where, in 1832, he established his own countinghouse in what was then a city built on mudflats. It would be another decade before the seven islands of Bombay were spackled together with silt dredged out of its six rivers; even then it would remain puddled with stagnant water that simmered year-round with mosquito larvae. The average colonial's life in India was said to span but two monsoon seasons, but the climate that felled Europeans posed no threat to David or his eight sons. Profits bought dock space in a deep-water port protected by the British East India Company. Family lore says David Sassoon spent nights with a pistol in his hand, shooting wharf rats overrunning his tiny warehouse. But no matter how modest his share, dock space allowed him the first pick of whatever came out of a ship's hold: spices, indigo, rice. Goods that made it to the marketplace were those he'd passed over. Once emptied, ships' holds filled with silks, pearls, and bolts of richly dyed cotton and wool. Within twenty-five years David Sassoon & Co. had branches in Hong Kong, Shanghai, Calcutta, and Canton. The farther east the Sassoons traveled, the clearer it became: success required them to suppress a family tendency to emotionalism. What was true in Bombay, where my grandmother's father became a British subject, would prove more so in Shanghai, where even the lowest among godown clerks were recruited from Baghdad. Chinese did business without facial expression, without gesturing, without any perceivable shift in affect. As put off as they were by Jews' excitability, so were Jews suspicious of their stilled faces.

"He never trusted the Chinese," my grandmother says of her father. "No one did, no one but a fool."

To the Sassoons—to all the Baghdadi Jews who presided over the Bund, turning money into money—a poker face that wasn't playing poker must be hiding something, and why would an honest man have things to hide?

Just as the *Encyclopaedia Britannica* cannot compete with the *Arabian Nights,* I cannot rid Baghdad of wicked djinns caught in lamps or Ali Baba's secret cave. I haven't been able to transport David Sassoon, secretly resplendent in his pearl-lined cloak, to Bombay other than by whisking him to its harbor on a flying carpet. And once a thing like a flying carpet gets into a story, it's impossible to get it out. Especially without anything to disprove or replace it. When I ask my grandmother how he got there, the answer is either "Now how should I know a thing like that!" or, more often, "Who do you think I am, Methuselah's grandmother?"

"Who's Methuselah?" I ask my grandfather. It's not a name on the Sassoon tree, I know that much, and I am my grandmother's sole grandchild.

"Noah's grandfather. It's a joke," he says when I say nothing.

Disdaining each other, the Shanghainese and the Jews with whom they did business were judged by the rest of the world as equally hard-driving and obdurate, one as likely to Jew a man down as the other.

Once the Crown had granted his company monopoly rights on cotton goods and silks, David Sassoon tried to convince the Chinese to trade cotton for tea, but the Chinese demanded silver, and Queen Victoria was not about to empty Britain's coffers to purchase tea. When the Treaty of Nanking gave the British access to Chinese ports, David Sassoon leapt to take advantage of what was already a brisk trade in opium, and established an office in Shanghai. Then he went to London with a proposition for Her Majesty: the export of opium, illegal in China since 1729, from the subcontinent to Shanghai, ships packed to the gunwales with sticky black balls of the stuff. In no time they'd have China at her knees.

"What do you mean they turned black?" My interest in opium is confined to my grandmother's description of the teeth of the American missionary's daughter Mabel.

"I mean they turned black," she says.

"Where did she get it from?" The idea of a missionary's daughter running amok in Shanghai is dizzying in its narrative potential.

"She paid one of the servants."

"A Chinese?"

"The gardener."

"What happens when you smoke opium?"

"I told you, your teeth turn black."

"But what else?"

"You get sent home to America."

By 1880 the Sassoons had a 70 percent monopoly on the entire opium trade. Next to—and east of—the Rothschilds, they were the richest Jews in the world. The remaining 30 percent was also controlled by Baghdadis: the Kadoories, Hardoons, Ezras, and Abrahams, among others.

Jewish opium merchants coerced Bengali farmers to grow poppies to the exclusion of rice and other food crops and took advantage of the British military to dispatch all Chinese who dared to refuse the opium. Middle- and upper-class Chinese, who had money to spend on vices, were dragged from their homes and into the street and forced at gunpoint to smoke the Sassoons' opium—firearms having been supplied by the British military. By the time my grandmother was born, in 1899, the British East India Company had staged enough public executions to firmly establish an addiction that exemplified Mao's condemnation of destructive Western depravity.

The Sassoons may have had a monopoly on opium, but opium did not have a monopoly on the Sassoons. Because my grandmother descended from Benjamin rather than his older brother, David, her side of the family had neither the immense wealth of David's direct descendants nor the responsibility for fostering an addiction that crippled an entire nation. Her father sold rubber and rice futures. There was money enough, and it wasn't tainted. No matter how great David Sassoon's humanitarian works, how many synagogues he built, how many hospitals and schools, every-thing he gave to the Jews was purchased with a disregard for Chinese lives. In any case, my grandmother's and my discussion of a centuries-long conflict-riven history involving every nation that did business in the treaty ports is confined to the missionary's daughter's teeth.

BAGHDAD TO BOMBAY, Bombay to Sydney, Sydney to Hong Kong, Hong Kong to Shanghai: an attenuated queue of Baghdadi Jews passed through Australia every year, a few pausing to take Ashkenazi wives to lighten what would otherwise be the dusky faces of their future children, an ambition satisfied by my grandmother's sister, Cecily. But not by my olive-skinned grandmother, with her father's Ottoman eyes. The brides were descendants of convicts, many of them—one of my grandmother's forebears is said to have been exiled from London to New South Wales for stealing a clock—but the color of their skin had the power to whitewash the past as well as the future.

As reported in the *Sydney Morning Herald,* on October 6, 1896, Solomon Sassoon Benjamin married my grandmother's mother, Miss Dollie (Rebecca) Cohen, at the home of Dollie's sister Anne Isaacs. (Arthur Isaacs, Anne's husband, would become my grandmother's guardian after the deaths of her parents.) Anne had been an intimate friend of Solomon's first wife, Fanny, who died when they were married but a year, giving the impression that Anne had taken it upon herself to undo Solomon's premature transformation into a widower. Four years had passed, a long time for a man hoping to start a family. He was thirty-three, Dollie twenty-six. He imagined she would outlive him.

"The ceremony was performed on the lawn under the

crimson canopy brought from the Synagogue . . . The bride looked well in rich white brocade, profusely trimmed with chiffon, a coronet of orange blossoms, and tulle veil." Her "four pretty bridesmaids" (three sisters, one friend) were dressed all in white, with "large picture hats with white plumes, and carried bouquets of crimson roses . . . Soon afterward, the happy pair took their departure for Katoomba, en route for a trip which will include Tasmania and Queensland before starting on their voyage for Hong Kong, their future home."

My grandmother at seventeen, standing between her parents. Her sister, Cecily, is in the background. Lake Hakone, Japan, 1916.

Département
des Alpes-Maritimes

REPUBLIQUE FRANÇAISE

MAIRIE DE ROQUEBRUNE-CAP-MARTIN

Arrondissement de Nice

EXTRAIT des Registres des Actes de Décès

Le *quatorze mars* — mil neuf cent trente quatre *deux* heures *dix* —, est décédé *en son* domicile, *Villa Egerton* — *Solomon Sassoon-Benjamin, rentier* né à *Baghdad (Turquie d'Asie)* le *vingt quatre mars mil huit cent soixante trois* fils de *Sassoon Benjamin* — et de *Saltsa Benjamin* — *époux décédés, veuf de Rebecca Cohen* — Dressé le *quatorze mars* — mil neuf cent trente quatre *onze* — heures —, sur la déclaration de *Jean Baptiste Calvy* — *soixante six* ans, profession de *Sous Directeur de la maison Roblot* domicilié à *Menton* — qui, lecture faite, a signé avec Nous, *Pierre Ostini, Médaille Militaire, Croix de Guerre* maire de *Roquebrune Cap Martin* —

24 March 1863

N° 13

Sassoon Benjamin

Solomon 14 March 1934

JB Calvy

No.	When and Where Died.	Names and Surname.	Sex.	Age.	Occupation and claim to British Nationality.	Residence at the time of Death.	Signature, Description and Residence of Informant.	When Registered.	Signature of Consular Officer.
295	1931 seventh March Château Mer et Mont[n] Menton	Dollie Sassoon BENJAMIN	female	60 years 7 month 2 days	wife of S.S. Benjamin born Sydney Australia 5 August 1870	Château Mer et Mont[n] Menton	S.S. Benjamin Cowdray, Villa Egerton Roquebrune Cap Martin	1931 ninth April	C. Belcher British Vice Consul.

I, *Charles Belcher*, British Vice Consul at *Menton*, do hereby certify, That this is a true Copy of the Entry of the Death of *Dollie Sassoon BENJAMIN* — No. *295* in the Register Book of Deaths kept at this *Vice* Consulate. Witness my Hand and Seal, this *ninth* day of *April* 1931.

Chas Belcher
British Vice Consul.

The family remained in Hong Kong for three years; Cecily was born there in 1897, my grandmother two years later, in London, where the family paused for some months while their new home in Shanghai was being readied to receive them for what was, to hear my grandmother tell it, a twenty-year purgatory before they came to rest on the French Riviera. Until then the family never lived anywhere they intended to stay; even when at "home" in Europe they split their time between Cap Martin and London, where they kept an apartment at No. 19 St. James's Square.

Katoomba, in the Blue Mountains of New South Wales. The island kingdom of Tasmania, not yet a state of Australia. And at last the Gold Coast of Queensland, prefiguring the Riviera, where death would do them part in another villa overlooking a different sparkling sea.

Already Dollie had renamed her husband, who from that point forward would introduce himself as Dick, just as the family would celebrate Christmas rather than Hanukkah while remaining kosher with regard to food and going to temple on the high holy days. If my great-grandfather couldn't be visibly assimilated, his Old Testament name could be disappeared, confined to official documents, like his death certificate, signed in 1934 by the coroner in Cap Martin. "Of a broken heart," my grandmother says whenever she speaks of it, as her mother died before her father, in 1931. But really he had a cerebral hemorrhage.

"WHAT'S THE MATTER?" I ask after the girl follows me through the foyer and into the living room, where she drops her satchel and covers her ears with her hands. She's not my friend but a classmate who got stuck going home with me because her mother's car broke down, a girl whose name I won't remember, only that she had black, bobbed hair and

was astonished to learn that I didn't have any Barbies.

"How do you stand it!" she cries.

"Stand what?"

"The ticking!"

I shrug. "I guess I don't hear it unless I try."

"They're broken, you know," she says later in the afternoon, when they all start striking not quite on the hour, interrupting home-work. "They're supposed to do it together." She leans across the table between us and speaks with slow emphasis. "All of them at the same time," she says. "Otherwise why would they be clocks?"

There's no reason to answer what I know isn't a question. It would have been different if she'd come home with me three months ear-lier, just after Mr. Cruikshank, who belongs to a guild of master clockmakers, had cleaned

and synchronized them. But in the manner of
mortals, the aged clocks fall out of alignment,
each taking its slow turn for the worse until
Mr. Cruikshank returns. Like a doctor, he carries a Gladstone bag filled with delicate tools.
I'm not supposed to be underfoot, but I can't
not watch as he turns their ancient faces to the
wall and opens the backs of their heads. The
stately, severe grandfather in the foyer is so
tall, and Mr. Cruikshank so small and stooped
he has to climb a ladder to see inside. Then the
two mantel clocks, the younger's white enamel
cheeks crazed with cracks, the elder's bronze
face dulled by the sweep of time's dirty hands.
And at last the carriage clock on my grandmother's nightstand. Even as other things van-

ish, the clocks, having conspired with my grandmother to
tick me backward, linger.

Because for some time now things have been disappearing. I go to school and return to bare floors. Who wouldn't
believe in flying carpets when only those without holes manage the trick of flying away? In fact, the holes are the proof of
it, preventing flight just as they sink ships.

Tables and chairs walk off in
the night. The delicate marquetry
nightstand on my grandmother's
side of the bed, legs as fragile as
a fawn's, vanishes out from under
the carriage clock, which remains
squatting on its gilded platform
as it migrates from one room to
another, never settling. Chests of

drawers evaporate, their contents relocated to overfilled closets. Paintings come down from the walls, leaving inside-out
shadows—ovals and oblongs absent of grime. The safe-
deposit box at the bank has vomited up every last jewel.
Suddenly the only Ming thing left is a vase with a visible
crack. Even our housekeeper, Tina, leaves, in a torrent of
tears. Emptied of her possessions, her little room off the
kitchen looks even smaller. Still we face impending ruin. As
we have no choice but to pay real estate taxes, there is next
to nothing and then nothing to pay for upkeep. No matter
where we hang on this trajectory, it is by the skin of our
teeth.

Mr. Cruikshank never speaks as he works, and I am
silent too, as I don't need to be told he's not the kind of adult
to indulge a child's curiosity. But he looks too much like the
drawing of Rumpelstiltskin in my edition of *Grimms' Fairy
Tales* for me to stay away. The crooked shanks of his name
climb onto rumpled stilts and won't come down. It's possible
he's a goblin. The longer I watch him, the more certain I
grow. The way he reaches into his bag with his long-nailed
fingers and without looking withdraws the exact tiny tool he
wants: there is something unnatural in this ability. When
he leaves, he picks his way carefully around the worn Persian
rug that lies just inside the front door, avoiding putting so
much as the tip of his pointy black shoe on it. Once, as he
was packing up his bag with his goblin fingers, I heard him
say under his breath, "Ring the bell, yes, come in, yes, and
then, just like that, crack, yes, head on floor."

The rug inside the door is small, only three by four
feet. Maybe that's why we use it as a doormat. I've been
asked, but I don't know the answer, why there isn't a non-
slip pad between it and the polished flagstone floor. Rou-

tinely, visitors, repairmen, and once, to my delight, the pediatrician enter the house, slip on the rug, and fall on the flagstone. My grandmother says nothing as she heaves them up, sits them down, and offers them tea. She calls this "mopping them," as if they were the floor rather than its victims.

Whoever it is, I can tell she judges the mishap to be that person's own fault, a faux pas often made worse by its being a first impression.

"TELL ME ABOUT your hair, about how long it was, and how the barber cried."

"My mother cried."

"You said the barber did."

"Well, if he did, it was because my hair was so thick it broke his scissors."

"Tell me how long," I say. It wasn't until my grandfather went to school that he had his first haircut.

"All the way down to my tuchus, blond curls."

The idea remains impossible, no matter how many times I hear it. I try to pick up a girl's head's worth of hair to set over my grandfather's face, halted by not knowing what he looked like as a boy, only as a young man. More than any other photograph, I want one of this particular astonishment. But there are no pictures of my grandfather as a boy, none before the age of twenty-five, when he was far from London and had wandered into a land so strange and beautiful that he had to have a camera, because what if he were to forget, or years later think he'd imagined what he'd seen?

"Tell me again how old you were."

"I was still in short pants," he says by way of an answer.

"What is it called again, what your mother put on your bread?"

"To take to school? Schmaltz, which as you know is goose fat, and that was my lunch wrapped up in newspaper."

"Did you like it?"

"I was hungry, so I must have."

I don't say anything. A lesson lurks behind the little sentence. Food summons a strictness in my grandfather that nothing else can. The dinner table has become a test of character.

"What's the use in forcing her?" my grandmother wants to know. She can't divine what he's made me understand: that by a mystical transference, every bite I don't eat I have stolen from a hungry child.

I spill my milk every night, *every* night. I don't mean to, but my hand thwarts me, knowing there is no other way to make it go away. The vessel stands sweating before me, bearing the calcium my bones demand, blue-white and translucent, the color of naked cartilage. I used to like milk when it was white and opaque, but the same conceit that has landed me in tights and a tutu—that my mother can remake me in the shape of a sylph—skimmed away its taste as well as its color. To the right of my plate, to the left of my plate, a glass, a tumbler, a mug with a handle: it makes no difference, I knock it over. It seems unreasonable, a *folie à trois,* that every night my grandparents and I conspire in a preventable disgrace, but I cannot bring myself to ask for it to be taken away. If I do, the cup of an African starveling empties before he can tip it to his lips. Either way, it drains away, as here my grandparents align with my growing bones.

"And I had to walk to school, an hour there and another back."

"Even though you were a little boy?"

"I went with my brother."

"He was only a year older."

"Nineteen months."

I don't need a photograph to see the boys, four and six, making their way through the London streets, so small they are waist-deep in fog, no taller than the wheels of the horse-drawn trams. It's impossible to get the damp out of London. The cobbles can't always be slick, the sun must shine every once in a while, but I can't make it break through the clouds. Only a soft drizzle of coal dust floats down, like static before my eyes.

"It was a little school called Marylebone School, for boys and girls."

"If you had short pants, did you have tall socks?" I ask.

"Knee socks, just like you wear to school."

"Tell me about the little girl."

"There was a fence separating the schoolyard, as girls and boys played separately, and there was a knothole in the fence, and we used to leave each other notes there, in the fence."

"They were love notes."

"Yes, love notes—tucked in the little hole."

"What did she look like?"

"She had red hair."

"What did they say?"

"I imagine they said, 'I love you'—what else?"

"They could be compliments. You could say you liked her red hair."

After two years at Marylebone School, my grandfather was six and sent to live away from home at Tivoli House, a boarding school exclusively for Jewish boys, in Gravesend, Kent.

"How far away?"

"It was about forty miles outside London. Three," he says, before I can ask him again how many times a year he

Tivoli House today.

got to go home to his mother. I've asked him if six isn't too young to go away to school, but he says he guesses it wasn't, and then he tells me my favorite story, the one about the policeman and the conker. One day, when he is outside with the other boys, he is caught throwing sharp stones at a horse chestnut tree, trying to knock a conker off a branch. The chestnut's trunk grew outside the wall around Tivoli House, but its boughs reached into the schoolyard.

"We tied them to the end of a string. Then you and the other fellow swung them at each other, and the one whose conker broke first lost. Anyway, as luck would have it, just at that very moment a policeman was passing by—"

"Did he have one of those tall hats bobbies wear?"

"Yes, that's what the stone hit, his helmet. He came into the school and told the headmaster that one of his boys was throwing stones into the street, and the headmaster assured him that such a thing wasn't possible, not from one of his pupils. But when they checked, sure enough, there I was, caught in the act. Boy, was that a caning!" My grandfather whoops with laughter.

"You didn't hit him on purpose!" I say, outraged each time he tells the story. "You didn't even hurt him if he was wearing a helmet!"

"What if it hadn't been a policeman in a helmet? What if it had been a little girl like you, looking up at the tree?"

"It still wouldn't be fair! Even if she went blind it wouldn't be fair." I feel no allegiance to this hypothetical child who complicates what is simple.

"Tell about the penny. Say what you bought with one penny."

"My dinner."

"And?"

"A haircut."

"And?" I say.

"Maybe a postage stamp."

"Or maybe ice cream."

"Or maybe ice cream," he agrees.

Cecily to the far left, my grandmother to the far right.
Cecily's lovers are between them.

MY GRANDMOTHER'S SISTER, Cecily, visits and brings
one of her lovers, the reviled Mlle. Garrigues, with "desperate rings of kohl around her eyes." The other stays home in
Nice and sleeps alone in the bed all three share, her name
eclipsed by "the Jordan Almond," as she has, according to
my grandmother, a face like a Jordan almond. Although she
is a native of Tunisia and sometimes referred to as "the Tunisian," the Jordan Almond is "a small and dubious-looking
Moroccan." Whether Jordanian, Tunisian, or Moroccan, she

doesn't exist in the albums or among the loose photographs. By 1922, when the family moved to the Riviera, my grandmother's lens had strayed from Cecily. Released from the claustrophobic community of the International Settlement, they went their separate ways. Cecily was more conspicuous in Europe than she was in Shanghai. Even in France, it seemed a little *de trop* to demand two women in one's bed. On the other hand, her misbehavior drew attention away from my grandmother, whose prematurely liberated view of sexual mores made her equally unmarriageable, at least within their caste. Like her sister, my grandmother was notorious for brazen affairs, but her weakness was men. One at a time, not two, but quite a few by the time she married. Several times, she tells me, her father—remembered by all for his patience and generosity—threatened to cut her off if—

"Off what?"

"If you cut someone off, that person no longer exists for you. Families used to send out black-bordered cards, like death announcements." She shudders dramatically. I'm sure she and her father both knew she'd never choose another man over him. But as a precaution, were affection found lacking, there was always the matter of her inheritance.

The most curious thing about what proves more visitation than visit is that Cecily and Mademoiselle share not only a bed but also chairs and dishes. At meals they perch on a single seat, left-handed Cecily on the left, right-handed Mademoiselle on the right. I set the table as my grandmother has taught me, doubling everything: knives, forks, spoons. The two women may take up a single seat and use a single plate, but the silverware fanning out from the sides of the one plate claims nearly two places at the table. When my grandmother comes to see that I've laid the forks and spoons down in their proper places, I ask if it wouldn't be better to put all of Cecily's silverware on the left and all of Mademoiselle's on the right, to prevent their having to reach across each other. My grandmother stares at the chair as if measuring its exact dimensions and how it will or will not accommodate two occupants.

"Well," she says at last, "I should think they could sort that out for themselves."

"May I change it?"

"Suit yourself," she says, so I do.

By association left-handedness has tethered my mother to Cecily, who it seems may have in turn bequeathed her lesbianism to my mother, just as my grandfather's sister Belle taught my mother to smoke when she was twelve. It would keep her slim, she said. My mother smokes Virginia Slims. If she is home at bedtime—this happens seldom—and if it is dark enough, she stands in my doorway and draws patterns in the air with the orange tip of her lit cigarette.

"Don't stop," I say. "Please?" But I can hold her on the threshold for only so long, and when Cecily and Mademoiselle visit she stays with them at the table, she doesn't come say goodnight at all.

Like the ominous bracelet from Ingrid, my mother's infatuation with Cecily forces the question of their affinity, some of which must serve a shared agenda to affront my grandmother. My mother looks more like Cecily than she does my grandmother, whom I resemble more than I do my mother, another of the unspoken divisions among us. Across an ocean, Cecily has insinuated herself into my mother by occult lesbian machinations. She has made her an unabashed Francophile, with an accent that is unnaturally Parisian for a girl who grew up in Los Angeles.

All Cecily and Mademoiselle's clothes are the same color—or it isn't any color at all, as everything's black—and they whisper together in French, lips to ears, largely ignoring everyone else at the table. I know not to stare but I can't drag my eyes off them, and my grandmother doesn't reprimand me. After dinner, when I carry their single demitasse, emptied of coffee, to the kitchen, I see that each side of the little cup bears stains of the same color lipstick.

From the kitchen, my grandmother says to Tina (who comes in one day a week and returns to wait table whenever we have company), first in French and again in English, loudly enough to be heard from the dining room, that Cecily and Mademoiselle are "the most frightfully shockingly beastly rude people on earth." She underscores this by translating a single word to French, *affreuse,* and repeating it twice. Eavesdropper that I am, French both tempts and repels me, as I am not sure I want to find out what my mother and grandmother say to each other and can tell more than enough from their faces, but by now I can't help but know some words, even if I turn my back on the grammar. *Affreuse, affreuse, affreuse.* Frightful, frightful, frightful.

My grandmother is in fact sufficiently scandalized to repeat the word throughout the rest of Cecily and Mademoiselle's visit. The word *affreuse* presages her arrival in a room and follows as she blows through it. Sharing a wingback chair, Cecily and Mademoiselle appear to have strolled out from Wonderland, elegant and lithe and not at all like the illustration of Tweedledee and Tweedledum in my edition of *Alice's Adventures.*

I understand why the rest of the family calls Cecily the troublemaker; it's nothing she does, it's just what she is. Also *soignée* and *charmante* when she wants. But she doesn't, like my grandmother, want to charm everyone or even anyone.

She is in fact like my mother, or my mother takes after her, beautiful and critical and waiting to be charmed. Even so, Cecily and Mademoiselle's visit provides an infusion of comedy, as in the wake of their departure my grandmother helplessly rehearses falling onto the couch with her hand clutching the part of her where she imagines her liver to be, crying out, *"Mon foie, mon foie! Chérie, mon foie!"* Her tone of alarm, emanating from the cloud of dust that even her 90 pounds can summon from the pink chintz, is the kind that accompanies a ready-to-burst appendix. I know this from the episode of *Daktari* I saw next door. The French, my grandmother assures me, are consumed by fears about their livers.

ELEVEN OH TWO SEVEN Sunset Boulevard. *Eleven oh two seven Sunset Boulevard. Eleven oh two seven Sunset Boulevard.* If I am ever lost, this is what I am to say. I sit on the ottoman in front of my grandfather's armchair and repeat the words until he is satisfied that I know them. The next day, and the one after, he quizzes me. The task of memorizing our address coincides with my introduction to memorizing phrases for Sunday school. But even if this were not true, the words amount to a prayer, something I repeat as I fall asleep.

"Who do I say it to?"

"A policeman."

"What if there isn't one?"

"You tell a grown-up, you pick one . . . one with a family, with children, like you. A mother or father who looks kind."

I nod. I know I will never forget the words, because I rehearse them silently whenever I am away from home and in the care of my mother, who forgets where she's left me or when to pick me up from a birthday party and has never forgiven me for once asking the birthday girl's mother to call the police to take me home. Along with my disastrous ballet recitals, which I beg her not to attend, it's a topic to which she returns.

"Anyone, even a two-year-old, would know better!"

"I was not a two-year-old!"

"Which makes it worse. Any eight-year-old would certainly know better!"

"I was five!"

She was already more than an hour late, my grandparents didn't answer the phone, and the birthday girl's mother was annoyed, I could tell. But nine-year-old me knows better than to say so.

There is a child my mother would prefer to have; she is her best friend Karen's daughter, Andrea. We're the same age and, forced into each other's company by our mothers' bond, would call ourselves friends. But my interest in Andrea lies in my mother's attraction to her. Andrea does not climb trees or get dirty. She is a willowy child who balances *en pointe*. Her hair is dark brown, like my mother's, and though my mother wouldn't say such a thing out loud, she doesn't have to: compared to me, as an accessory—like the perfect handbag to go with her shoes—Andrea is a superior complement to my mother. If Andrea were her child, they would go about the world pirouetting in matching dresses.

AT MISS ROBESON'S Academy for Young Ladies, my grandmother's father paid a surcharge so his daughters could have their own bathwater rather than share it with other girls.

"How many other girls?"

"Four, maybe."

"How do they all fit?"

"They don't. It's one at a time."

"But then whoever's last gets cold dirty water."

"Tout à fait," she says, and I see two tubs side by side, one filled with clean hot water, tendrils of steam rising from a crystalline surface, the other cold and gray and clouded with soap scum.

Shanghai has made my grandmother into a stickler for hygiene and a violent scrubber. Balanced on the edge of the tub, she proctors my baths, and after rubbing me raw turns the washcloth over to me with instructions to "wash down there, and do a good job." Her vehemence convinces me that whatever it is between my legs, I do not want to see it, this source of corruption she refuses to approach even with a hand protected by a *flannel*.

"How much did it cost?" I ask, thinking that under such Darwinian restrictions clean hot water might be expensive.

She doesn't answer. It's not the kind of thing—like my grandfather's lunch, haircut, and postage stamp that add up to a penny—she remembers, if she ever knew.

"Tell me something else." My grandmother closes her eyes while she thinks.

"Every three months a hairdresser came to singe the ends off the boarders' hair," she says.

"Singe like set them on fire?"

"Not fire, but burning them off, yes."

"Why wouldn't he cut them?"

"That's how he did it, that's all. The way it was done."

"What did he use?"

"Tongs."

"Tongs like fire tongs?"

"Smaller. Two flat metal pieces, with handles. Like a pair of scissors." She makes a snipping gesture with one hand, singeing the air between us. "He left them over the coals until they turned red and then he clamped it over the ends of our hair. Smelled nasty."

At Miss Robeson's Academy, the curriculum included elocution and something called "practical knowledge," which has "gone out of fashion."

"Is knitting practical knowledge?"

"Well, it is practical, but there were no knitting lessons at school."

"Did your mother teach you?"

"Oh no," she says, laughing, and in fact my great-grandmother was remembered as "delicate and useless," one cousin's description a fair representative of the general opinion. "I started during the war, when we were stuck in the Orient and bored stiff for years. By the time we got out, I knew how to play bridge and tennis and drive a car. I could fox-trot and speak French—"

"And Chinese."

"No, that's pidgin."

"What is practical knowledge?"

"Penmanship. Etiquette. I was always good at spelling." Infallible, in fact—I go to my grandmother before a dictionary.

"Say about the tooth on the pivot."

"How can you want to hear a thing a hundred times?"

"I do, that's all."

The tooth on the pivot is like my grandfather's long curls: its power lies in my not being able to picture it.

"Terribly intelligent but unable to impart her knowledge," my grandmother says of her arithmetic teacher, Miss Cuthbertson. It might as well be an epitaph, as she says it every time she mentions the name. Aside from being overly intelligent (my grandmother is disinclined to inflate the worth of academic pursuits), Miss Cuthbertson bore the misfortune of a tooth "on a pivot," which failed to hold it in place, so it fell out.

"And then," my grandmother says, "all the girls dove to be the first to find and return it to her."

"Why?"

"Well, we were getting terrible marks, most of us, and always looking for a way into her good graces."

"But a pivot is something that makes things go around. Why would a tooth be on one?"

"It was, that's all."

"It fell out just anywhere?"

"We never saw her anywhere but in the classroom. We flopped from our desks right onto the floor."

"How often did it happen?"

My grandmother shrugs. She is done with the tooth.

"MY FATHER WAS an accountant. That's how I got my jump on figures. I was always good at figures."

Like his father, Samuel, before him, and my grandfather, Harry, after, Emmanuel Jacobs was one in a line of math prodigies. Math was all any of them owned, but a jump on figures was a thing no one could take away. Emmanuel wasn't cooped up inside an office, though; he was described by the 1891 census as a "turf accountant," a bookmaker at Alexandra Park, the only racecourse within the city of London. His height was an advantage in what was understood to be a dangerous job, feeding as it did on a vice that left the afflicted at the mercy of debt collectors. Aside from organized criminals, mobs at the track were thick with pickpockets; bodyguards accompanied the more successful bookies.

I don't know what it's like, working at a track, and I don't understand how the bets work, but it's easy enough to place a tall handsome man in a crowd of short thieves, holding his money out of their reach, protecting his family's fortune, meager as it was, until he fell ill. After he died there wasn't a cent, only debts.

As soon as my grandfather turned fourteen, he was apprenticed to a cabinetmaker in Berlin, just as his brother, Sid, had been the year before. "My mother thought it would be good for me to learn the language, that it might help me when I got older. She wrote to a friend of hers in Berlin who had a factory, making furniture for the upper crust—"

"What's the upper crust?"

"People who can afford pearwood and rosewood, all inlaid with mahogany, all custom-made and hand-polished—it was very beautiful. I was an apprentice there, what they call a *lehrling,* and I got forty marks a month."

"Nana's upper crust." If inlaid mahogany is a measure of caste, it confirms my grandmother's status as royalty.

"Yes," he agrees.

"How much is forty marks?" I ask.

"Today it would be ten dollars, a little less. I had to get there at eight in the morning and I left at eight at night. I used to walk three miles each way, and I walked that trip four times a day, twelve miles. I left there at eight o'clock at night, and by the time I got to my lodgings, it was almost nine o'clock, and that's when I got my supper."

"Did you have lunch?" I ask.

"Yes, that's why it was four times a day. I walked back to my lodgings for lunch."

"Jack of all trades," my grandmother calls my grandfather, not without reason.

He was unhappy in Germany, and then unhappy in London, where the only respite from indoor clerical work was to be found in training exercises for the Royal Bucks Hussars, which he joined soon after returning from Berlin. A volunteer cavalry unit—much like the Army Reserve—based in Buckinghamshire, the Hussars put him on horseback for the first time. As he was with the unit from 1907 to 1910, between the second Boer War and the First World War, there was no fear of being sent to the front, only pleasure to be taken in getting out of the city on weekends and attending the annual summer camp. It was in the Hussars that my grandfather learned to ride, care for a horse, and handle a rifle while on horseback, skills he'd be grateful to have acquired before landing in the New World.

My grandfather, Talkeetna, 1915.

But first, London:

"Tell me them again."

"Tell you what again?"

"The jobs, all the jobs you had in London."

"Well, let's see. First the library, then the women's linge—"

"No, you have to say about them too. Go back."

He never says it's silly to ask him to recite what I already know.

"Well, of course, not knowing the names of so many of the authors, how long could I last in a library? I had to climb ladders up to the ceiling to get a book by an author I'd never heard of. I lasted a week there. Then I got another job, keeping books—"

"Different books from library books."

"Yes."

"Books of numbers about money."

"For a concern that sold women's nightgowns and

things, and I had a little petty cash there, so I used to buy the stamps for them, and I stuck that job out for six months, and I got sick of being indoors, so I told them I didn't like it and I quit."

"Now buttons and braid."

"Yes—another bookkeeping job, for a German concern. The salesmen there would write up their orders in a book—so many boxes of a certain kind of button and so many boxes of a certain kind of braid. I stuck that job out for a year, and I couldn't stand it any longer, being cooped up all day—"

"So you went out on the road."

"I said I couldn't stand being indoors, so they sent me out on the road."

"And what did you know about selling buttons and braid?"

"And what did I know about selling buttons and braid?"

I DON'T KNOW enough to call it perverse, but I recognize it for what it is.

My grandmother has given my mother copies of all her credit cards, along with instructions not to use them. My spendthrift mother, she says, is to keep them in her wallet in case of an emergency. She says this knowing that my mother's emergencies are shoes. There is always another pair she must have, there cannot be too many, and they cannot cost too much, and thus we are bankrupted and dunned.

Worse, my mother makes me her accomplice. "Just to see," she says, and she stops at Bullock's or Saks or I. Magnin on the way home from ballet, and straight up we go to designer footwear. She sits on black leather benches while princely shoe salesmen go down on bended knee to slip pair after pair on her Cinderella feet. It isn't her indecision that keeps us here for hours, it's that she is so happy in shoe departments, too happy to leave. Towers of boxes of rejected shoes climb around us. Occasionally one falls. The salesman is always indulgent and sometimes flirtatious. It's true she is beautiful, but my grandfather has explained how it is for a man selling shoes: patience pays off. By the time he has stacked the shoes my mother wants (and it's rarely a single pair) next to the cash register, I'm tired and hungry and desperate to get out of my leotard. I always have a book, as these stops happen more Saturdays than not, and history has proved that it is not possible to hurry my mother; she says it slows her down when I interrupt her to ask when we can leave.

I'm leaning against a warmly lit glass counter when it's delivered: the comeuppance my mother's financial "emergencies" predicted. Staring at the scarves and gloves inside and holding my nose because accessories are adjacent to perfume, with its predatory saleswomen who chase down shoppers to atomize clouds of scent over their skin.

"I'm sorry," the woman behind the counter says to my mother, "the account appears to have been closed. Perhaps you'd like to pay another way?" A silk scarf made by Pucci lies on the glass counter, appearing to float between them. I look up and see my mother's white neck color with embarrassment. Her pale, manicured fingers accept the defunct card, its shiny surface embossed with my grandmother's name, and slip it back into her black wallet with the gold interlocking C's.

It's a fast drive home. My sparkling mother crosses the threshold like a thunderclap, and just like that there isn't any air or light; there's noise, that's all. Things shatter. Doors slam; drawers do too, kitchen drawers filled with cutlery that clatters with every assault. My mother and grandmother scream at each other, often in French. My mother always smokes, and never tries to tap her cigarette over an ashtray but lets the ashes drop on the carpet. "It's good for the rug," she says as she rubs them in with the sole of her prettily shod pretty foot.

It is always the same fight, so predictable that there's no point in eavesdropping, and I know better than to remain in sight. My mother asks my grandmother how she could have put her in such a position, and my grandmother counters with the same objection: how can my mother have put her in such a position? Doesn't my mother understand that she has forced my grandmother to close the account? And how is it possible, really, to spend a thousand dollars on three pairs of shoes? My mother isn't so foolish as to answer this question by naming names: Maud Frizon, Charles Jourdan, Yves Saint Laurent.

When they stop fighting—nothing resolved, the cease-fire a result of exhaustion—my mother leaves, trailing smoke from a Virginia Slim as though set alight by rage. She doesn't kiss me goodbye; our leavetaking is the thud of her car door, which calls me to a window or out from behind a tree to watch her taillights disappear. The driveway is steep enough for this to happen quickly. Curiously—I find it so—I am always on my mother's side. I don't yet understand this for what it is: a matter of reflexive sympathy, what one feels for an underdog.

My mother, Carole Jacobs, at nineteen, sitting under the olive tree just outside her bedroom.

"THERE WAS A crank to turn the engine over," my grandfather says of his first car, and he tells me that in 1910 people thought it was unsafe for human beings to travel as fast as

twenty-five miles an hour.

"Nana drives eighty," I say.

"Does she?"

"Sometimes eighty-five." This is true—she goes ninety—but it's still the sixties, and the California speed limit is seventy.

"I don't mean to," she says. "Creeps up. Marvelous car." That the speed can creep up while the big Cadillac engine purrs is the measure of the car's marvel.

Upstairs in the library is a box of automobile club medals my grandmother pried off her Hispano-Suiza when she had to leave it behind in France, fleeing the occupation. And in the lockbox holding her papers and her father's pocket watch and fobs is a little gold medal for winning a race in the Italian Alps. It was 1929; she was thirty years old, her father almost sixty and preoccupied with the declining health of her mother. It was almost too easy to disappear for a week, unchaperoned. Half a day's drive from Cap Matin to Lake Como, where she stayed with him, whoever he was, at the Grand Hotel. Cecily's private life made public—a life performed for maximum impact—drew the family's attention away from her.

My grandmother counters any criticism of her speeding with a recitation of her driving skills, acquired in Shanghai when she was fourteen. "Oh, what tosh!" she says to the Department of Motor Vehicles official when he returns her failed written examination. "What unmitigated tripe!" It should hardly be a surprise, as she hasn't read, let alone studied, the California drivers' manual since the last time she had to have her license renewed. Maybe she's never read it at all. She looks up from

Medal from an automobile rally, St. Remo, November 9–11, 1929.

the graded test, gashed with red marks, and tells the young man on the other side of the counter that he wasn't even in short pants when she learned to drive.

We return to the DMV a week later, after I've studied the manual and quizzed her every evening after dinner. She sits at one of the desks in the cordoned-off test area, takes a cursory look at the multiple-choice questions, upturns her purse onto the dirty linoleum floor, and waves me over from the bench in the waiting area to catch and collect the rolling lipstick and coins. Or so I think. But when I approach the examination area, she shoves the crumpled test, camouflaged by a flurry of stray Kleenex, into my hands. "You take it," she whispers, too loudly. My protests are cut off by the approach of a suspicious DMV employee, at whom my grandmother smiles and waves cheerily, as if delighted to be chosen for a visit; it suggests her innocence, as what cheater would welcome the approach of a proctor? She explains to the towering woman that her granddaughter is helping her collect all that fell from her handbag—her wallet and keys and so forth.

"You're not allowed in the test area," the woman says to me, and I step back over the white plastic chain that surrounds it.

Minutes later I'm in the women's room, crouched on a lidless toilet, my feet on the seat, choosing among A, B, C, and D. I return the test as I received it, under a blizzard of tissues. The proctor shakes her head in exasperation as she walks toward my grandmother's desk. Upon arriving, she heaves an exaggerated sigh. My grandmother looks up at her.

"I fell in the bank last year," she says, inspired. She is telling the truth. "Just the same kind of floor as this. Slipped and broke my hip," she says, her implication clear: She doesn't want to risk such a thing happening again; that's why she called me over to pick up what she dropped.

A series of expressions pass over the proctor's face: irritation, incredulity, disgust, pity. They settle into weariness.

"Are you done, then?" she says, and my grandmother says she is. I escort her to the counter where the tests are graded. My grandmother, barely eye level with the counter, stands on her toes to hear the verdict.

"Marveeeelus!" she cries when we pass, the drawn-out *eeeee* a measure of delight. We did not get a perfect score, because it struck me as provocative to do so; I made a deliberate mistake.

"Thank you, darling," she says in the parking lot, her

new temporary license snug in her wallet, and she makes me promise not to tell my grandfather. "It would be wrong if I were a bad driver," she says as she starts the engine. "But we both know I'm not," she adds, as she knows he is less liberal than I with regard to my grandmother's ethics, which dovetail with her desires.

"I won't," I say. "Tell me about the real test."

Every time she tells the story, something's added on. So far she has navigated a flock of sheep and a sea of rickshaws. She has traversed the great Bund, been up and down and down and up it; she has driven to the racecourse, attaining such narrative velocity that I see her tearing through the bleachers and onto the course, scattering horses.

According to my grandmother, the Chinese are devoted gamblers.

"I don't understand why there would be sheep in a city."

"Well, there were, that's all."

"Was there a shepherd?"

"I was driving, not interviewing the natives." My grandmother's tone makes it clear that all she says must be weighed and considered; she is not a reliable source of information about Shanghai, not its history, culture, or inhabitants, or even its streets, buildings, and banks on the Bund. She swears the yellow river was named Whangpoo because it is a cataract of sewage, and across the river is Poo Dung Point, where excrement collects.

"Look at a map, why don't you?" she says when I ask if she's sure. "I didn't make up the names."

She drove the length of Bubbling Well Road, all the way across the city from the Bund, and back past the public gardens with the sign that said, NO DOGS OR CHINESE IN THE PARK. She drove around the old city, and past her

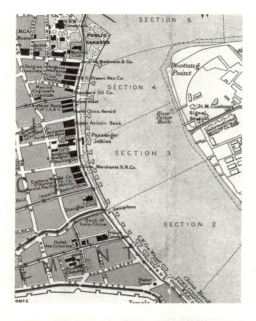

Elly Kadoorie and his sons, Horace and Lawrence, in 1917.

father's brokerage at the intersection of Jinkee Road and the Bund.

Benjamin, Kelly, and Potts opened in Hong Kong in 1902. Within ten years it had become the premier brokerage in Hong Kong, with offices in Shanghai. Owned in partnership by my great-grandfather, S. S. Benjamin; Ellis Kadoorie ("Elly" to family and friends, "Kelly" for business); and a Mr. George Potts, known to all as "the silent partner."

"Why was he?"

"I would think that would be obvious."

"He must have said something in all those years."

"He was a widower," my grandmother says, seeming to imply that grief had rendered him mute.

Elly Kadoorie had followed the same trajectory as Solomon Sassoon Benjamin, leaving Baghdad in 1882 for Bombay, where he

became a British subject, and working in London before settling in China. Among the three men, only Elly Kadoorie
would continue to magnify his fortunes; only he had sons
as heirs.

"They burned down the police station," my grandmother says.

"Who did?"

"The Chinese. Louza Station. Threw stones at the
police."

"Why?"

"I don't know. There was a lot of unrest."

"What do you mean, unrest?"

"Riots, kidnappings. That kind of thing. They all had
to have their queues off—those who refused were chased
down. They tried to hide them under their hats, but then
hats were abolished too."

My grandmother makes it sound as though it were
nothing but haircuts and haberdashery, but when the 1912
abdication of Emperor Puyi left China in chaos, it wasn't
in hidebound Peking that nationalist and communist fac-
tions lunged for power but in unapologetically capitalist,
Western-gazing, forward-thinking Shanghai, whose taipans
found themselves in a position to recoup fortunes lost in
the rubber crash, and where Sassoon employees, of which
there were scores, were routinely kidnapped to shake down
ransoms from the rich Jews responsible for weakening the
proletariat with opium, among other Western perversions.

"What else?" I ask of what must have been the longest
driver's test in the history of the automobile—not official.
No license was required to drive in Shanghai, not when it

Monsoon season, Shanghai, 1920.

was a treaty port. A test of the wily chauffeur's devising. Perhaps wily enough to take my grandmother on the most challenging—maybe he hoped the most discouraging—of throughways that parted herds of livestock, leaving the car "absolutely filthy!"

Unwashed wool is, my grandmother tells me, not a pretty sight.

"What else?"

"A Chinese wedding."

"A wedding in the street?"

"Any excuse for a parade. The noise—you have no idea."

The noise. The filth. The heat. The noise. The filth. The prickly heat. The filth. The Paris of the East is a litany of discomforts and dangers. Every impediment to civilized life. Chinese urinate and worse in streets of mud. Native children's trousers don't have proper crotches but are split open, their private parts made public, so they can squat and do their business wherever they please. Cholera, typhoid, meningitis. Rabies, yellow fever, malaria. Insects, snakes, intestinal parasites of all kinds: most go to your brain or strangle your ventricles or eat your aorta. Green Gang gangsters, Bolsheviks, opium addicts, missionaries. Jews from pogroms. Drunkards, beggars, lepers, and harlots of every stripe. Peasant women run down the street while nursing children run along beside them, their mothers' nipples caught in their teeth.

"Pulled out as long as razor strops," my grandmother says of the mothers' breasts, and as my grandfather has a leather strop, I suffer the misfortune of being able to picture this all too well and know it is a thing not even she could invent.

But the noise of a Chinese wedding is a thing unto itself. There is nothing like it, as it partakes of riotous theater

The juncture of the old Chinese city and the French Concession.

audiences, traffic jams, garrulous tea parties, firecrackers, gongs, bells, drums, and jackhammers—an unimaginable cacophony.

The finale to a musical may be no better than "a Chinese wedding, I tell you, an absolute Chinese wedding."

Birds conduct Chinese weddings under the feeder. A restaurant may be unworkable due to reasons of Chinese weddings going on all around. On occasion my grand-mother has collected me from a mismanaged birthday party that has run amok into a Chinese wedding. She stands behind me in the foyer as I curtsy and shake the mother's hand and say, "Thank you for having me, I had a lovely time." When I hear her accent acquire a heightened plumminess, I don't have to see to know the smile that accompanies it—altitudinous to the point of being frigid. But if she holds herself above schoolmates' parents, it's no higher than I hold her myself. I know it to be ill-bred and vulgar for the birthday girl or boy to open presents in front of their guests, rather than after the party is over. I know this just as I know American children are not *brought up* but *dragged up,* an expression conjuring an image of myself flanked by my grandparents, holding tight to their hands and wearing Mary Janes that never get close enough to the ground for the crisscross to wear off the soles. The three of us are walking into the future, silhouettes against a sunset. Falling ever farther behind us, my classmates' parents pull them along by the scruffs of their necks, their heels drag-ging in the dirt.

The roads weren't paved in Shanghai; they were dust, they were mud, they were rocks and potholes. Some had soft shoulders over which cars rolled and toppled into the filthy filthy filthy Whangpoo—no one understands this kind of filth, it's a thing even a person with the descriptive powers of my grandmother cannot convey. The city swarms with dirt that is alive and malevolent. A microscope would find it bubbling with protozoa. In fact, mud is lethal worldwide, boiling with roundworms and hookworms and pinworms, too many worms to keep track of them all, and my grandmother allows me to go barefoot only on the lawn or on the beach, which is clean because saltwater and sun kill germs.

"What does it mean if a car doesn't have a key but a crank?" I ask my grandmother.

"It means the chauffeur stands in front of the car and turns a crank until the engine starts." I nod. I've seen this happen in cartoons.

"But not the Hispano-Suiza," I say of the car her father bought her when they moved to the Riviera, an occasion she recounts each time with fresh excitement as though it had just happened the previous day.

"Here it is . . . *not!*" her father called up the stairs—by all accounts, he was a great tease—and down she came, "at least five times," to discover that her car had not yet been delivered.

We both picture her tearing down the villa's staircase and through the salon to throw open the door on the empty street.

"No, that had an electric starter. This was the horrid Bentley we had in Shanghai. Beastly rotten shock absorbers. Jam jars. Pitched like a boat. There wasn't anyone who didn't feel sick in that car."

"Jam jars?"

"Shaped like."

"What were?"

Villa Edgerton, Cap Martin, my grandmother's home from 1922 to 1934.

"The shock absorbers! They looked like enormous jam jars."

It occurs to me that my grandmother might know quite a lot about automobiles. "Can you change a tire?" I ask.

"Twiddle a few bolts around and there you have it."

My grandmother in 1925, with her first car.

"GOD IS ALL-IN-ALL. God is good. Good is Mind. God, Spirit, being all, nothing is matter. Life, God, omnipotent good, deny death, evil, sin, disease. Disease, sin, evil, death, deny good, omnipotent God, Life." I copy the words over and over until I can recite them by heart, but what I regurgitate makes my head spin. I try to get through Sunday school the way I spell *antidisestablishmentarianism* aloud for my grandfather, by breaking Christian Science into pieces that, taken together, add up to something, but the only thing I am confident I understand is that my body is a figment of my imagination and the number of times I get strep throat a measure of my wickedness. I've asked my mother if she believes in her body, as it was her idea for me to become a Christian Scientist, but she's not the sort of person who feels obliged to keep up her end of a conversation.

Once my grandfather understands that Sunday school is so abstract as to be useless, he takes it upon himself to install my moral compass. He begins by driving us to where Santo sleeps in a garage beside a lawn mower. Santo works for Diego. Once a week Diego leaves Santo and the lawn mower on our driveway, and Santo pushes the mower back and forth over the grass until Diego comes back to fetch him. Diego doesn't pay Santo; he gives him what passes for room and board in exchange for his labor.

A thin mattress covered in stained blue-and-white tick-

ing lies directly on a concrete floor. Next to it is an over-
turned apple crate with an overripe banana on top.

"Is that Santo's dinner?" I whisper, although there's no
one to overhear. Not even the lawn mower. It's the middle
of the afternoon; Diego is driving Santo around in the back
of his pickup. As Diego bills his clients directly, the only
money Santo ever sees is what my grandfather surreptitiously slips under the crate.

"Is it?" I squeeze my silent grandfather's fingers. "Do
you think Santo doesn't want a pillow or Diego won't give
him one?"

We're walking back to the car and I'm trying to sort out
what's worst, the mattress, the banana, the smell of gasoline,
or the fact that there wasn't a toilet Santo could use, when
my grandfather says, "What are you going to be in life, a
giver or a taker?"

I don't answer. We both know it isn't a question.

THE HOUSE WAS in danger before it was built, in 1950, on a foothill missing its toe. Sunset Boulevard, racing down from Hollywood and hurrying west toward the Pacific, had lopped it off. Then, to make matters worse, my grandparents had the toeless hill topped to make a flat surface on which to build a house and plant a garden. Before plans were drawn or foundation dug, my grandfather began setting sprigs of ice plant into the bank that drops precipitously onto Sunset Boulevard, facing the cars that speed past. No sidewalk divides the street from the houses. The driveway, a hairpin

11027 Sunset Boulevard, 1951.

turn carved into the hill's west flank, is graded to a stark 30 percent, enough to give visitors pause as they tilt the hoods of their cars up a steep incline whose end is not in sight. After they park in the circular driveway, some get out with a look of triumph; more are pale and gone in the knees, the malicious carpet in the foyer lying in wait.

"Why ice plant?"

"Because it has deep roots that stop erosion. And it's drought-resistant."

"So that's all, just roots, that keeps the house from sliding down onto the street?"

"That's all," my grandfather says from behind his newspaper. He lowers it to look at me. "I did work on the railroad, you know. I was an engineer."

As I believe he knows everything, my grandfather's nonchalance about a hill held together by roots dispels my anxiety. The new picture I have of the lowly groundcover with its purple flowers draws inspiration from *The Little Prince,* whose towering baobab trees hold the prince's planet together. There's a word for what my grandfather is, although I don't know it yet: *autodidact.* If he's not reading history books, he's reading biographies—of Winston Churchill, Teddy Roosevelt, John F. Kennedy, Albert Schweitzer, Mahatma Gandhi, Albert Einstein, lives as thick and heavy as bricks—or the newspaper, or listening to baseball games on the radio.

He teaches himself how to graft fruit trees; he makes a fishpond from chunks of pink quartz and other rocks from the California desert—obsidian, tourmaline, chalcedony— with a copper crane at one end, its beak pointed up to spray a fountain of water over the pond's surface. Koi swim with their mouths above the water, open so wide I can see down their throats. I'm the one who gets to feed them, and the one who cleans up when I accidentally pour the whole can of pellets into the pond, nearly choking the fish to death. It's not a punishment; I'm crying too hard for anyone to want to teach me better. My grandfather shows me how to drain and refill the pond.

"Inevitable," he says, after we replace half the clouded water with fresh and find a fish lying on the driveway, gills stopped, scales shining like a new penny against the wet blacktop. "Got past the screen. One always does somehow." He digs a little grave in the garden and drops the fish inside, covers up its bright scales with dirt, extinguishing them.

"Will it turn into a flower?"

"Zucchini, more likely." He grows too many zucchini, far more than we can eat ourselves. As with avocados and lemons, it's difficult for a guest to leave without a bag of them. A few just lie there on the warm dirt, getting bigger and bigger until they are picked to become edible cooking vessels, which my grandfather cleaves in half, guts like a fish, and stuffs with something I'm guaranteed not to like and will be forced to eat. In the end, it's V8 juice that settles the question of whether I can accurately divine what will make me, as my grandmother calls it, "violently ill," an expression whose inherent drama amplifies the shame of it. But as I complain to my grandfather, his usually dependable sympathy disabled by his having grown up hungry, it takes too many ruined dinners to prove my point. Even my tears do not move him. Because I always cry when I throw up. School, home, public, private: I weep to have made so clear and undeniable an announcement of the wickedness within me. I have fallen into error, lost God's company.

In response, I follow a trajectory opposite to that of most children, growing into an ever pickier eater, not only regard-

ing new foods with suspicion but also refusing to eat anything I've ever thrown up. V8 juice, Wheatena, egg salad,
tomatoes, hamburgers, hot dogs, plum pudding, cheese
fondue, pineapple, green Jell-O, red Jell-O, orange Jell-O.
Jell-O.

"You have to try a thing at least once," my grandfather
says, presenting it as an ethical obligation, which for him
it is.

"Why is it a victory garden?"

"You could call it a kitchen garden."

"But you said *victory*."

"The first one was. It was part of the war effort. The
more people grew what they ate, the more of the public food
supply would be available for the army. There was even one
at the White House."

"That was the first garden you ever had, when you were
fifty?"

"First time I stayed in one place long enough to keep a
garden."

"When you married Nana?"

"When I married Nana."

"Sing," I say when he falls silent.

My grandfather's sisters, Belle and Violet, made what
living they could in music halls, sometimes performing
together, sometimes apart, and rehearsing at home. By the
time my grandfather left London, he knew scores of popular
songs, some of which I know by heart, so often has he sung
them to me. I wouldn't recognize a Beatles song, I don't
know who the Doors or the Monkees are, only that they all
amount to tests I have failed by asking other children ques-

Harry Samuel Jacobs, 1942.

tions like "Who is Davy Jones?" questions that don't elicit answers but echoes. *Who is Davy Jones? Who is Davy Jones???*

There is no limit to my ignorance about rock and roll, just as there is no end to my grandfather's vaudeville repertoire, nor any bedtime that doesn't end with "Just a Song at Twilight," *when the lights are low, / And the flickering shadows softly come and go, . . .*

The lyrics slow; they drag my eyelids down. Slow until the words part, one from another, *Though the heart be weary, sad the day and long*, and I step through them as easily as Alice does her looking-glass, step through the song into twilit London, where shadows gather around the bright circle that falls on the cobbles from the tip of the lamplighter's wand, and the flickering dead follow the flame he carries from one streetlamp to the next, and I run after him too, over the slick cobbles, through the fog, trying to catch up to the light.

I'm not asleep, I'm not awake. I feel my grandfather kiss my forehead, and I let him go. I can't not pay heed to the dead, can't not run after Emmanuel Jacobs.

I never catch him. I have no face to give him, only long legs to outpace the coaches, from London to Brighton and places.

"OH, I DON'T know!" my grandmother says as I wait for her to remember something she hasn't yet told me about the Trans-Siberian Express. "You know there was a piano in the dining car."

"Yes, and no one ever played it, and a library and salon, and it took eight days and you went with your governess but not the amah, and there were camels in western Siberia. Which was just yellow lakes and mud and lost camels."

"Who said they were lost?"

"Aren't they supposed to be in the desert?"

"Siberia is a desert."

"But it's covered in snow," I say.

"Underneath it's sand, just like the Sahara."

"People live in yurts."

"Yurts?" my grandmother says.

"Round tents."

I know this because we're among those families who cannot discard back issues of *National Geographic.* Instead they are stacked in a closet behind the sofa upstairs, out of order and some so old the covers have fallen off. The closet smells of dust and so do they. I page through them languidly when I'm bored, look at the pictures.

"Well, there's this," my grandmother says, uninclined to make anthropological observations. "We got out at—oh, where was it, Irkutsk? I can't remember, but it was where the track gauge changed, and all the passengers had to get off the train. Cecily and I played in the fresh air. I thought everything would be white, but the locomotive left black soot on the snow, and a cinder blew from the stack into my eye."

"Did it burn your eye?"

"No. It was cold by the time it floated down. I was looking up, you see, watching the snow come down. It didn't snow in Shanghai, not more than a few flakes."

Pictures suggest that trips "up-country" from Shanghai and the two or three months my grandmother and her family spent in Japan each year offered plenty of diversions, romantic and otherwise, but according to my grandmother, the single silver lining to World War I was not having to take an eight-day train ride to school.

"*Tomsk! Omsk! Tobolsk! Ilka! Shilka! Chichma! Ufa! Zagladino! Abdulino! Ust-Katav!*" The stationmasters whistled their loud whistles and called out the names of the stops.

"It sounds more like a magic spell than it does like stations."

"Magic it was not."

There are not enough details about this mystical train that crosses the frozen steppes and delivers its passengers to Red Square; there cannot be enough for me. The stereoscope card from the box upstairs in the library, the twin images of St. Basil's Cathedral tinted to suggest what *National Geographic* reveals as blinding colors and striped turrets, onion

domes with gold crosses on top—it looks like what Disney-
land pretends to be.

"Are you sure you didn't go there?" I ask.

"I was going to school, not sightseeing."

"It wouldn't be sightseeing, a place like that. You
could go between getting off one train and getting on the
next." Because that's what they did: from Moscow, the girls
and their governess disembarked from the Trans-Siberian
Express and boarded a wagon-lit for Paris. From there it was
on to Calais, and, after being seasick all across the Channel,
another train from Dover to London, where they attended
Miss Robeson's Academy for Young Ladies.

My grandmother looks at the stereoscope card and
hands it back to me. "For all I know, our governess bought
that in the Moscow station."

There are other Russian cards as well, a few of the railway's construction, serfs swarming like ants over avalanches
of snow, dragging what's too heavy to carry, and one of a
black locomotive boiling over with black smoke and pulling
a string of coaches out of a storm of white, the track, like
the end of the train, invisible. The czar and his family have a
private train; each car looks like a room lifted from a palace
and put on wheels.

"We passed right through that dreadful town," my
grandmother says.

"What town?"

"Yekaterinburg. Where those poor girls died. Four of
them, and that poor little prince, their mother and father."

"How did they?"

"The Bolsheviks shot them."

"Why?"

"King George refused them asylum in England. They

looked so alike, people confused them, George and Nicholas. First cousins. Anyway, George refused to let them take refuge in England. So they died in a basement in Siberia, all seven of them, and their servants."

"But why? What did they do? Why did—what are they called?—why did they shoot them?"

"Bolsheviks." My grandmother sighs a theatrical sigh, projecting boredom, to remind me to address political questions to my grandfather.

"We were in Shanghai during the revolution," she says, and she tells me the city was flooded with destitute White Russian refugees, titled princes who, one after another, fell in love with what they expected my eighteen-year-old grandmother to inherit.

"Why were they white?"

"Why were what white?"

"The Russians."

"Because they weren't red."

The answer is confounding, and my grandmother is not interested in explaining why red Russians stayed at home, in their own country, and the white ones ran away to chase her around Europe as well as China.

"**TELL ME HIS** name again."

"Michael Evlanov. He ended up marrying Elizabeth Arden," she adds, her tone familiar, as though she knew the founder of the cosmetics empire personally, the two vying for his hand. In my grandmother's stories, Prince Michael— Mischa to her—is by turns ridiculous and dangerous, lurking about the South of France, waving pistols and threatening suicide and embroiling my twenty-five-year-old grandmother in a compelling tangle with her father, who promised to cut her off if she married the nefarious gold-digging bounder; their chauffeur, who threatened to blackmail my grandmother, knowing as he did when her whereabouts were wrong; and an unscrupulous maid who worked the night shift at the Hotel Le Negresco.

At the time my grandmother was living with her parents and sister in the family's villa overlooking the Mediterranean Sea in Cap Martin, where her family had moved from Shanghai after the First World War and her father's subsequent retirement. Villa Edgerton, as it was called, had a secret bar behind the library's

Prince Michael Evlanov, circa 1940.

The view from the terrace of Villa Edgerton, 1925.

bookcase, which sprang open with the press of a button under an adjacent shelf. The house had a secret stairway as well, the kind that encouraged what my grandmother calls "assignations."

"How many servants?" I ask her.

"Oh, I don't remember. No Chinese, obviously, and—"

"And no Sikh police."

"No Sikh police."

"You must have missed them."

"I did not."

"I would have."

Sikh police wear turbans like snake charmers', only red. They are imported from what my grandmother calls British India, as she has not relinquished her standing as a subject of the empire upon which the sun does not set. Both my grandparents have suns that never set, as my grandfather ascends to the endless days of the North Pole, and my grandmother follows the equatorial middle, around and around the same world.

"Let's see," my grandmother says, returning to my original question. "We were long past governesses. The usual, I suppose: butler, housekeeper, cook, two ladies' maids, a valet, a footman, parlormaid, downstairs skivvies and scullery maids. How many is that?"

"How many skivvies and scullery maids are there?"

"Oh, say three altogether."

"What's the difference between them?"

"Neither get as far up as the parlor."

"I'm asking what's different, not the same. Anyway," I say when she says nothing, "it's eleven." I've been counting on my fingers. "But you forgot the chauffeur, so it's twelve."

My grandmother makes a face. Nearly forty years after the fact she is still angry with the chauffeur.

My grandmother, gazing directly at the camera, with her mother, on the left, and Cecily quarreling in the backseat. The impassive chauffeur was their driver in Japan, 1918.

Mimi Hayim, 1925.

There are many versions of how my grandmother's affair with the prince ended—a multiplicity of what she would call "three sides to every story: his, hers, and the truth." I'll hear them years later, from various members of her family, and while some details change from one retelling to the next, no one leaves out the pistol. Although my grandmother's cousin George Hayim says it was his mother who waved it.

"Mimi! Mimi Hayim with a pistol!" My grandmother laughs until she collapses onto the couch. "The sight she was back in Shanghai, cycling along Bubbling Well Road. If only you could have seen her, just exactly like an enormous stag beetle on a bicycle!" Whatever my grandmother's aunt Mimi does, it is as *an enormous stag beetle*. All her dresses were black bombazine, and the antlered hats were black as well. "To draw the eye away from the rest of her," my grandmother says of the hats. "If ever there was a quixotic enterprise. Why a woman of such magnitude would get on a bicycle is beyond me."

"Maybe she rode it so a rickshaw man wouldn't have to pull her?" My grandmother has told me that Cecily always got out of sedan chairs when they came to a hill.

My grandmother doesn't answer. She is laughing too hard about the bicycle. When she recovers enough to speak, she tells me what I'll learn for myself one day: George routinely tells lies about his mother; it's something of a hobby of his, or a party trick, to see how outlandish a story he can

tell—or perform with dramatic abandon—without arous-
ing the suspicion of his audience.

The first time my grandmother got out of the limousine at the Hotel le Negresco and told the chauffeur he was
free for the night, she didn't require transportation home,
he only half understood the opportunity it presented him.
Because she couldn't be spending the night with a lover,
could she? No one was so brazen as to live in Cap Martin
and conduct an affair in Nice, only fifteen miles away, at a
hotel celebrated for the sort of guests tourists crane their
necks to glimpse: Italian aristocrats and Polish royals, stage
stars, divorcées, millionaire tuberculars in rooms with bal-
conies from which they could dip their wasted hands in the
turquoise sea, and Nellie Melba, who took to bed there after
her farewell tour, eating eponymous toast.

The second time, he stalked around the grounds, slipped
through the lobby, and found where the maids and waitstaff
took their breaks. He'd thought of bribing the concierge or
the man behind the front desk, but the obvious choice was
someone from housekeeping, an employee with less to lose.
He'd picked her out already, careworn, down at the heels.
Whatever was wrong—a sick child, a laid-up husband, or
maybe just bills—he knew she'd do it. All he needed was a
photograph.

The third time the chauffeur dropped my grandmother
at the Hotel Le Negresco he drove the car around the corner,
parked it, and returned to the hotel. In one hand he carried
all his savings, in the other he held a framed photograph of
my grandmother.

"Nicked it off the piano," she says.

"I want to know who Miss Benjamin is meeting," he told the maid. "Whose room is she spending the night in?" The maid hardly glanced at the picture before she gave it back.

"She's not the kind you forget," she told him, and asked him how much.

Expecting to barter, the chauffeur named a figure half what he was willing to pay. She agreed to the price without argument.

"I'll wait," he told the maid. And wait he did, for seven hours. He was asleep in the limousine when she knocked on its window at three in the morning. By the time he'd driven back to Cap Martin, it was 4 a.m. When he picked my grandmother up at noon, he waited again, but only until he'd driven her half the way home. Then he told her what he'd learned and how much it would cost her to keep him from sharing it with her father.

"He knows," she said from the seat behind him.

"He knows?"

"My father knows I am with a lover. So there's really nothing for me to pay you for."

"He knows his name?"

My grandmother didn't answer. The chauffeur stewed for a day before calling her bluff.

"What is his name?" her father asked him.

"Evlanov. Prince Michael Evlanov."

"Thank you."

"Is that all?" the chauffeur asked.

"No," my great-grandfather said, but instead of producing a checkbook, he told him to pack his things: he was fired.

Evlanov answered my great-grandfather's summons eagerly, mistaking its politeness for warmth and imagining he was about to be embraced as a son-in-law. Instead my great-grandfather, as dark as the prince was white, asked him who was paying for his room at the Negresco.

"Who?" the prince echoed.

"Yes," my great-grandfather said. "Who?"

"Now how should I know?" my grandmother says to me when I ask, and claims she has no idea how the rest of the conversation unfolded.

Whatever was said and by whom, Evlanov, having been sent packing, returned in the middle of the night with a pistol he said his great-great-great-grandfather had carried during the war of Polish succession and threatened to commit suicide if he was separated from my grandmother.

"A flintlock or some other nonsense. It misfired," she says.

It misfired through his foot. It misfired through a window. It misfired and killed a pet monkey. It misfired and . . . whatever it did, my grandmother makes sure I understand, it did not do it because an enormous stag beetle pulled the trigger.

"So that was it?" I ask.

"I should think it would be enough."

"LET ME SAY them," I say, and I list the places from east to west. "Quebec City, Fort William, Winnipeg, Kootenay, Tête Jaune, Prince George, Prince Rupert, Juneau, Anchorage, Talkeetna." No reason to resist wanderlust when there was always a bookkeeping job waiting in the town ahead, and if not that one, the next.

Once back from Berlin, my grandfather stayed in London as long as he could stand it—three years as it turned out—moving from one job to another, as he would for years hence. His brother, Sid, fell in "with a bunch of kids that were . . . anyway, a bit unruly, and—"

" 'Bad influence.' That's what you said before."

"And my mother thought the best thing that could happen for Sid was to send him abroad, so we financed him and we sent him to Canada, and he landed in a little place called Fort William, on Lake Superior, and he tended bar there—"

"And he started sending you pictures of fish."

"One picture of this beautiful lake, where he caught big fish—six and eight pounds on the hook!—and that was it. I couldn't stand it any longer, so I said, 'Mother, I think I'm going to have to join him.' So she cried bitterly and didn't want me to go."

Whenever my grandfather's mother cries, it's bitterly. She has suffered what other people haven't. But she always helps my grandfather; she "puts others before herself." I know this isn't a physical act, and yet, as I listen in the dark, I see all the people she puts before herself congregate in her boardinghouse kitchen; too many, they spill out the doors, front and back.

"My mother got together twenty pounds, and relatives helped, and I went to Canada. I think the fare was seven pounds, and I was on the ship eight days, steerage."

"Are there windows in steerage?"

My grandfather laughs. Apparently not only were there no portholes, because steerage is below the water, there weren't even rooms, only hundreds and hundreds of bunks and straw on the floor, so it sounds like a floating barn.

Steerage is a word my grandmother uses to indicate any misplacement of herself, who is accustomed to first class. The context is never nautical: a bad theater seat, the wrong end of a dining table or the back end of a restaurant, a hotel room "miles" down the hall from the elevator. Any of these is "Steerage!" Sometimes "Siberia!" or "Timbuktu!" But mostly "Steerage!"

In the New World, my grandfather never stayed any-where for long. He loved math but not the kind that kept him indoors, which it didn't when he was surveying or working as an engineer, both of which he says he "picked up" with his jump on figures.

"Cut and fill," he calls what he did, moving dirt from one place to another. Moving himself from one place to the next. When he didn't quit, he got fired, once for something as silly as singing a song.

"What was it?"

" 'I love, I love, I love my wife, But oh you kid.' Popular. Anyway, the guy I was keeping books for, he heard me and thought I was flirting with his wife, who was working in the office there alongside me, and that did it. He fired me on the spot.

"It was really something," he says, laughing. "Couldn't keep a job! Never lasted more than six months anywhere!"

It was weeks more often than months. But his voice is unashamed, even delighted. He liked to move on and continued west until the land ran out, in Prince Rupert, British Columbia.

"And you flipped a coin in Prince Rupert."

"I flipped a coin in Prince Rupert."

"Heads for north and tails for south."

"Heads for north and tails for south," he agrees.

"And it was heads."

"It was heads."

"So you went to Juneau."

"I got a job in Goldstein's Emporium, as bookkeeper. It was three stories high—a skyscraper!" He laughs. "So old man Goldstein sold furs, and he used to send his son way up into the arctic regions, the fur-bearing area, to buy pelts from these trappers, and I heard from old man Goldstein's son they were going to start this railroad from Anchorage up to Fairbanks, from Seward to Fairbanks. I said, well, it looks like there's opportunity for me."

"So then you were—"

"Then I was in Anchorage, where the ships came in offshore and they had lighters that transported the freight onto the mainland."

Juneau, 1917.

"What's a lighter?"

"A lighter is a little boat. Anchorage had a deep port, but it was a ways out from the shore, so small boats—lighters—had to carry the freight. The U.S. government had started to draw plans to divide up the land. They were setting up to sell lots and make a town of it. All these foreigners were coming in, and all these railroad workers. It amounted to a couple of thousand people. The Alaskan Engineering Commission needed someplace as a distributing point. So they surveyed these lots and they sold them off, and that was Anchorage."

"What's a commission?" My grandfather pauses; he draws in a breath and holds it for a few moments, the way he does when he's thinking up an answer I'll understand.

"President Wilson, Woodrow Wilson, decided to have a railroad built from Anchorage to Fairbanks, so he appointed a group of people to oversee—watch over—the building of the railroad."

"And that's a commission, people who watch over something?"

"In this case."

"Tell me about the Indians."

I am uninterested in cowboys, fixated on Indians.

"I kept on with the surveying party for the Alaska railroad, and they sent me to this little Indian settlement, Talkeetna, where the rivers converge—"

"The Talkeetna, Susitna, and Chulitna."

"Talkeetna, Susitna, Chulitna. I kept books for them there, the AEC, all the supplies coming in on these scows, flat-bottomed boats. The government didn't have to buy new equipment—pile drivers, steam shovels, what have you. Those were shipped all the way up from Panama—the canal was built by then."

"Say about the mosquitoes."

"Summer, they were so thick we ate at the mess table with veils on. Like beekeepers use. I used to lift up the veil, put something in my mouth, and pull the veil down. And this was with a smudge in the center of the table, that's how thick they were up in Talkeetna."

"What's a smudge?"

"It's burning punk in a—"

"What's punk?"

"Rotted wood, never really catches, only smolders, so it makes a blanket of smoke to keep bugs away."

"What did the Indians do about the mosquitoes?"

"Who do you think taught us how to make a smudge pot?"

"What else?"

"Well," he says, pausing to think of something he hasn't yet told me. "One tanned a big black bear hide for me, which I'd—"

"Is that the biggest trap?"

"A bear trap? Yes. Steel-jaw trap." I say nothing.

"We put them out of their misery straightaway," he says, and he tells me he never trapped alone, only with a partner, as it was dangerous for a man to trap by himself. The Talkeetna had their own special way of tanning, he says, by beating the skin a great deal, and then after they'd beaten it they used alum and eucalyptus to make the hide soft; otherwise it would dry stiff and hard.

"What's alum?"

"A chemical, looks like salt crystals. Pulls the moisture out, keeps the hide from rotting. So this Indian, he had this knack of doing it, so he did that for me, and I also asked him to make me a cover for my shotgun, and he made me a most beautiful deer-hide cover with strings of beads all down it. Beautifully made."

"What was his name?"

"Now that's a thing I can't remember," my grandfather says after thinking a moment.

"What about Six-Mile Mary?"

"What about her?"

"Tell me!"

"Six-Mile Mary was an Indian woman, a hundred and six years old. She had about ten or twelve kids, and she smoked—"

"A corncob pipe!"

"That's right, and to fill it with tobacco she had to walk three miles into town and three miles back—"

"So they called her Six-Mile Mary."

"So they called her Six-Mile Mary."

Six-Mile Mary at her camp, three miles from the town of Anchorage, 1918.

"**WHAT IS A** sponger?" I ask my grandmother after George leaves. George is my first cousin twice removed. One warm spring day, he arrives without warning in a floor-length mink coat. Like my mother, he uses the *f*-word. Half the year he lives at the Plaza Athénée in Paris. As for the other half, my grandmother says, he could be anywhere. "What's a sponger?" I ask again.

"Guests who never depart, as they haven't any money to live on."

"George left."

"I wasn't talking about George, but his . . ." She settles on *companion.*

I don't know what *homosexual* means—it's a word I've never heard, as my grandmother's *idée fixe* does not include men—but I do know George will never be a father, because fathers don't wear floor-length mink coats in warm weather or live in Paris at the Plaza Athénée with their mothers, entertaining handsome young spongers.

"Is George rich?"

My grandmother doesn't answer; I am being inquisitive, and worse,

Cousin George in the Royal Navy.

about money. Besides, she is preoccupied with being scandalized by George's coat and expletive and annoyed at me for liking him as much as I do.

George is in fact so rich that he has never worked a day in his life, and has acquired his wealth from his father by means of blackmail.

"Here's how it is, sweetie pie," he tells me years later, when I'm old enough to know, the two of us sitting across the dining table in his Paris apartment. The apartment's walls are a *trompe l'oeil* mural of the ruins of a Greek temple, broken columns lying all about us. In the center of the table is a silver punchbowl bearing a mountain of white granulated sugar from which the handles of at least twenty-five sterling spoons protrude like porcupine quills. His refrigerator is filled with butter, whereas my grandmother stacks butter in the freezer. The fear of running out of butter, and an emphatic preference for Irish butter, is a family preoccupation.

"I refused to stop meeting men in the public toilets across the street from his place of business until he paid me a certain amount of money, not a penny less. And so he did. He was a cruel man—no one liked him, not even my mother. Especially not my mother. He kept a long pin in his lapel, like a hatpin, and once when I said a thing he disliked—I can't remember what—he ran it through my lip." He touches one finger to the middle of the bottom one. "For a long time I thought he'd come up with the idea himself, but apparently it was a common punishment in Baghdad."

Once upon a time, George was a mad young thing who cultivated Gore Vidal, Jean Genet, Princess this and Duchess that, and movie stars. Now he doesn't bother. At eighty, George is "your fairy godmother, sweetie pie!"

He takes on the role of Babar's Old Lady, marching me up and down the Champs-Élysées, to Lanvin, to Chanel, to Hermès.

"Take your time choosing," he says outside the glass doors to La Maison Guerlain. From one block to the next he has tried to educate me about perfumes, a crash course amounting to three principles: most fragrances are execrable, some are tolerable, and the very few without flaw are made by Guerlain.

The saleswoman in the *parfumerie* greets George as "Monsieur Hayim!" and kisses both his cheeks before asking an underling to bring him a chair.

"Mitsouko?" I ask. George shakes his head violently.

Serge Marquand, Princess Ercolani, David Niven's son, Mrs. Niven, Roger Vadim, David Niven, Deborah Kerr, and, in the center, cousin George, Klosters, Switzerland, 1958.

"Absolutely not! Not until you are much, much older!"

"Jicky?" I try.

"Not really you, is it, sweetie pie? Too insouciant."

It takes a great deal of time and scores of white paper wands dipped in one art deco bottle after another before the exhausted saleswoman and I wash ashore, hanging tight to L'Heure Bleu.

As my untrained olfactory apparatus has made one mistake after another, George selects for me, and tells me *l'heure bleu* describes the liminal sky, caught between day and night, an invitation for lovers to meet, no matter how briefly, as the light ebbs.

When I try to stem the cataract of gifts that flow into the traveling case he says I need (in lieu of my own, which is *pas possible*), he makes a moue and calls me mean for "not allowing an old queen the few pleasures left" him. So here we are, laden with shopping bags, on the threshold of yet another boutique, where I allow him to buy me a long blue evening jacket but not the matching trousers, as they seemed to add up to entirely too many francs, even to me, notorious for misplacing decimal points when making currency calculations. The next morning he looks at me across the breakfast table and says he cannot believe "how absolutely idiotic" he had been to listen to me. "Asinine!" The day's first order of business is to return to purchase the trousers.

"You know I'm right, sweetie pie. I was lying in bed all night wondering what on earth you could wear with that divine jacket, and there is only one answer. The trousers that go with it." The current sponger smiles at me from the kitchen.

George's spongers are never the louts he claims he wants

but kind young men who are gentle with him. "I can't get anyone to tie me up, sweetie! I'm serious, it's very distressing." His problem is, he says, that he only wants to be with heterosexual men.

"Why else, really—think about it, sweetie pie—why on bloody earth else would I join the navy if it weren't for all those brutes stuck on a ship without a woman in sight?"

I am staying with George when the current sponger prizes a mushroom of distressing proportions from the trunk of an oak growing by the side of the road. The current sponger is married to a woman who has left him to live with her identical twin, the only person who understands her. He was returning to Paris after an unsuccessful attempt to win his wife back when he saw the mushroom.

"Tripes de chêne!" George cries when he sees it in his arms.

"Something off an oak tree?" I ask.

"Tripe!"

It looks like an asymmetrical human brain and weighs ten pounds—a fantastical size that sets George looking for a cauldron. A mushroom like this demands homage. It cannot be shaved away slowly, it cannot be frozen or wasted. The sponger ought to have considered the inevitable result of his actions. There is nothing to be done but have a party, a luncheon that segues into dinner, the centerpiece of which is a mushroom risotto that has the preternatural quality of seeming, as the hours go by, not to diminish, despite everyone's having second and even third helpings. The party begins at noon and ends when the last guests depart, at midnight, when George changes into his pajamas in front of the stragglers. Until then an animated clot of ten or twelve guests moves one way and then the other up and down the immensely long blue table (it matches the *trompe l'oeil* sky above), claiming clean settings while George and I clear those of guests who have departed the same way they came in: through a large window onto the back alley.

"All those locks—I can't be bothered to answer the bell." George lives in Montparnasse in one of those flats that open onto a locked courtyard, and leaves the window open with an upturned box beneath it for guests to use as a stair. Once over the sill, they step into one of George's stories about his mother, who was born "on St. Helena, only a hundred or so yards from Napoleon's house. Being a small sweet pretty child, she was invited to play with Napoleon's tortoise. They became dear friends, and when Napoleon died, she inherited the tortoise, which she took back to England, where it lived to be one hundred and died only because my mother had died the week before and the smell of death sent the tortoise on to its own—"

One guest finally interrupts what the rest have been enjoying. "Oh, George, do shut up. Your mother can't have been born until seventy years after Napoleon died."

"Oh," George says mildly. "She must have told me the story wrong."

George Hayim at eighty.

Before I leave, my new traveling case packed and most of the clothes I brought with me confiscated—"For the impoverished," George says—he gives me a photograph taken on his eightieth birthday. "The wings were a gift, so I had to try them on, and as I wasn't wearing anything that went with them, I took it all off." He takes the picture and studies it. "You must admit, sweetie pie, I do look wonderful for a man of my age."

THERE ARE A lot of words in Christian Science, but they don't add up to stories or even pictures, only teach me that "malicious mesmerism" from unseen forces can strengthen the "inharmonious body" that preys on my own unwitting flesh.

As far as I understand this, I have a wicked doppelgänger who feeds on my flaws and misdeeds. Invisible, like the portrait hidden in Dorian Gray's schoolroom, she reveals my diseased nature, summoning strep throat that will not cease believing in itself until I manage the trick of not believing in it. I know that as my five physical senses do not take Spirit into account, they are to be ignored for the liars they are, but I am stubbornly incarnate and have yet to figure out how to navigate the material world without them. Stuck with my chronically infected tonsils, in which the pediatrician believes, and inured to shameful symptoms, I don't aspire to disbelief. Instead I grow addicted to fevers high enough to lift me out of my grandparents' big bed, where I lie during the day so as to separate it from the night. Impatient to break through the trembling threshold of 104 degrees, as soon as I'm given a chance, I take matters into my own hands. No one suspects I hide the chewable orange tablets of baby aspirin in a crumpled tissue until I can drop them into the toilet. Who would guess that as soon as it's safe to assume the rest of the household is preoccupied by teatime,

I strip off my nightgown and, wearing only underpants, slip outside into a downpour? I run through the needling rain to the biggest tree in the garden, an old avocado I have claimed as the best for climbing, its broad thick leaves forming a hollow canopy under which to hide. Arms around my knees, teeth chattering, I crouch on its fallen leaves to watch rain pock the surface of the fishpond, waiting for chills to shake my temperature up. Everything looks like an eclipse, burnt out in the middle, ringed with white fire. I have no sense of doing anything ill-advised to a body whose corporeality I am encouraged to overlook. It's too late to save myself from Christian Science, the only part of whose doctrine I can discern and use is the equation drawn between physical disease and "error."

Seven, eight, nine years old, I have mastered, almost, the mortification of my flesh. Everything is a test. Vise, pliers, hammer. My grandfather would weep to see me at his workbench. The one time he catches me doing something "silly"—for what child would hurt herself on purpose?—the shame it inspires, enough to make my cheeks burn, does not teach me that I am doing something wrong. How else am I to learn to separate myself from the body that betrays me, announcing to the world that I am a bad child, when all I want, with all my heart, is to be good? How else but practice the art of ignoring what's only another case of strep throat? Instead of going back to bed and doing what I can to get well, I wait to return to the house until I've gone where thermometers don't measure the state of my soul, only confirm that I've arrived where water drips green off the wet leaves and flowers change color like chameleons. The wind knocks unripe avocados from the tree; fruit hammers the ground. The climb from 104 to 105 degrees is no different from a plummet down a rabbit hole, an abrupt change in altitude that delivers me to a place where the rain's black pocks arrange themselves in patterns, cover the pond's surface with runes that shimmer, charged with significance. The koi open their round mouths and sing carols, and angels float overhead, bearing messages on ribbons of gold that unravel from their mouths.

Imps, pixies, goblins, Pinocchio, Abraham Lincoln, walking on water, centrifugal force, alchemy, Atlantis, unicorns, dragons, ghosts, appendicitis, rabies, tuberculosis, snail fever, the philosopher's stone, Rikki-tikki-tavi, the Elephant's Child's nose, Noah's ark, ruby slippers, genies in lamps, the curse of the pharaohs, flying carpets, Red Riding Hood's grandmother in the belly of a wolf, Bluebeard, Sonny and Cher, Doctor Dolittle, hobbits, Alice's looking glass, the six wives of Henry the Eighth, fauns, centaurs, mermaids, vampires, witches, hemorrhages, guillotines, Mr. Ed, talking trees, setting fires with a magnifying glass, stigmata, reincarnation, werewolves, Aztecs throwing girls into volcanoes, UFOs, Laura Ingalls Wilder, Lazarus, leprechauns, magic wands, *Apollo 11*, the Phantom Tollbooth, the Loch Ness Monster, Santa Claus, Saint Peter at the gates of heaven with the real list of who's naughty or nice, Osiris's feather of truth revealing whose heart is heavy with sin: I believe in everything and investigate what I can.

Unlike Mary Poppins's, my grandfather's big umbrella fails to carry me into the sky on an updraft; it pops inside out on the way down from the garage roof. On the other hand, a magnifying glass can set dry leaves on fire. "Only on the driveway," my grandfather says, and he tells me not to teach the neighbor boys how. Avocado leaves are the best, tough and dry and woody enough that they catch slowly. I have to hold my hand absolutely still to sharpen the sun into an unwavering hot pinpoint. A black hole appears, and a filament of smoke curls out of what opens like a tiny eye. I squat on the driveway until my legs are numb and tingling, trying to burn pictograms into the leaves.

Taken as I am with strange fancies, I am an obedient child who gets into mischief no one can predict or, therefore, prevent. Like all of Christian Science's troubling abstractions, malicious mesmerism will never assume a form more palpable than gravity, a thing so familiar I don't sense its presence.

IT'S ALWAYS HAZY in my Shanghai; a "noxious effluvia" rises from the sluggish yellow river. Shanghai was filthy with the kind of filth that required an army of coolies to beat back from the Benjamin-Sassoon estate. Behind its walls, my grandmother's family subsisted on imported staples and fruit and vegetables they grew themselves and, once picked, washed with carbolic soap. They kept livestock shipped from England—Buff Orpington chickens and Guernsey cows. They carried smelling salts, which my great-grandmother needed after she saw a Chinese pastry chef employed by the Astor House Hotel unroll a sheet of dough on his unclothed, unwashed, sweating belly. My grandmother still carries them in a tiny flask of amber liquid, but I'm the only one who opens its lid, not to revive myself but to revisit the burn in my sinuses and how it rises into my eyes and makes them tear. She also carries squares of gauze soaked in rubbing alcohol and sealed in foil packets to scour the receivers of public telephones should she be forced to use one, and to disinfect the silverware should circumstances force her to patronize an untested restaurant. It's mostly not funny, the filth, blamed for the death of my grandmother's baby brother and her mother's descent into permanent neurasthenia. I'm scandalized by stories about the *kongs* that rolled by each morning to collect what fattened up their drivers' rice paddies. My grandmother swears that one of their servants fell into a *kong* and died of fear before she had a chance to catch a disease.

"How did she?" I want to know.

"How did she what?"

"Fall in."

My grandmother shrugs. "I suppose she must have been carrying out the chamber pots," she says.

Shanghai, where my grandmother's family of four commanded more than fifty servants: an English butler, head maid, and cook; a Scottish governess; Chinese valets and Chinese chamber, laundry, parlor, nursery, and scullery maids. Forty coolies, half of whom worked outside the house.

Filthy, filthy, filthy: my grandmother never says the word only once. Not when Shanghai is the topic. To eat anything grown outside the walled garden was considered an invitation to, if not a guarantee of, cholera. Death.

Like many children in the International Settlement, my grandmother and her sister had not only a governess but also two amahs to do the governess's bidding. Many of the stories my grandmother tells include amahs chasing after children with articles of clothing. It wasn't until my grandmother was in boarding school that she learned how to dress herself and button her own shoes.

"Say it again? Please!"

Missy Peggy, Missy Peggy, you are messink your boot!

It was the amahs' responsibility to provide the first defense against contagion. *"Missy Peggy, Missy Peggy, no touchee! No touchee! What you belong, fooloo girl? Wanchee catchee dilolee?* Peggy, Peggy, don't touch! Don't touch! What's the matter with you, are you crazy? Do you want to catch dysentery?" The Chinese amahs couldn't pronounce the letter *r*. That's how my grandmother became Peggy instead of

Margaret, which is how she signs her name, in a curious penmanship, different from what marched along the top of my second grade's blackboard. Where I am forced to make points, she can use smooth curves.

AS SHE HAS every school night of my life, my grandmother sits at the kitchen table with my white saddle oxfords placed neatly in the middle of a page taken from the newspaper and uses a rag to spread Hollywood Sani-White over the scuffed white leather. After it dries, she buffs them until they shine; at least they do on the way to school. I come home and kick them off without unlacing them, scuffed gray.

Me, in the fourth grade.

"I can do it, Nana," I say, watching her fingers, their joints swollen from arthritis, but she says no, she likes to do it, just as she likes to pull my hair back so tight my eyes water and scrape my scalp with the barrette I remove as soon as I am out of her sight.

"Her hair is always in her face," the teacher tattles, and my grandmother laments the fact that I cannot, like my mother, look like I "stepped out of a bandbox," an expression I mistakenly attach to marching bands rather than clerical collars kept clean in a box.

"Say something else."

*"You wanchee catchee one piecee rickshaw for walkee godown?"** *

---

* "Would you like me to call a car to the warehouse?"

Yangjingbang Creek, 1910.

Pidgin was a language of commerce, a hybrid of Cantonese and English; the pidgin particular to Shanghai was called Yangjingbang, as the creek of that name, dividing the French and British Concessions, was a meeting place for Chinese and Western businessmen.

"Say 'upstairs, downstairs.'"

"Topside, bottomside."

"Say—"

"What fashion no can talkee plopa?"

"I don't want to talk properly. I want you to teach me all the pidgin you know."

"I don't remember all the pidgin I know."

"Tell me again the word for what your father was. *Tinkeeman?*"

My grandmother laughs. "No, that's an intellectual."

"Like Cecily."

"Yes." My grandmother makes a face that says intellectuals are tedious. *"Taipan,"* she says. "My father was a *taipan.*"

AS GENESIS AND Revelation are the only books of the Bible that Mrs. Eddy, as we are taught to call the founder—discoverer—of Christian Science, cared to unlock, I ask my sometimes babysitter, Libby, to explain what happens in the Gospels, only snippets of which we have read in Sunday school, as if any more than a verse might confuse or intoxicate

Libby holding my mother, 1943.

us. Libby, whose real name is Vera Libbin, was once my mother's governess and slept where I now sleep, in the yellow room down the hall from my mother's. She never leaves her apartment without little folded tracts with JEWS FOR JESUS printed on the front with a blue Star of David in place of the *o* in FOR. She doesn't hand them out; she leaves them on bus seats. Wherever we go, and it isn't ever anywhere but to the La Brea Tar Pits (because, I suspect, neither of us knows how to get anywhere else), we change seats as many times as possible, leaving tracts behind us.

The tracts are the kind of secret that, if told, would end in Libby's being scolded, not fired, or "let go" as my grandmother says, as if releasing someone from the trap of employment. Libby is more a member of the family than she is a babysitter; I am the only child she cares for. Although one day, sitting beside her on a bus, I have an epiphany: seeing how the black orthopedic shoes that boost her two inches closer to five feet dangle even further from the floor than my red Keds, I understand that it is my responsibility to protect Libby, who looks much less substantial out in the world than she does when in her tiny apartment.

We never go into the museum at the La Brea Tar Pits, not after the first time when I read the plaques aloud to Libby, explaining how prehistoric mammals fell into the tar, sank, suffocated, and left their stained skeletons behind, like the saber-toothed tiger and woolly mammoth on display, their brown bones wired together so they make sense. La Brea Woman, an Indian who fell in 10,000 years ago, couldn't be rearticulated; she's just a few ribs and a blackened skull. It's the tar itself that we come back to see, over and over, each of us hanging on the chain-link fence around the oozing acrid pools to watch as bubbles of gas slowly rise to the surface and linger, their black skin growing thinner and thinner until it looks clear. Then it pops. We time them with Libby's wristwatch. Once a big one took almost a minute to slowly emerge and burst.

We quarrel once, and never again. My grandmother drops me off at her apartment, and I come in with a big bag of lemons, two dozen at least, from my grandfather. There's no reason for my petulance, but there it is. As I set the bag down I sigh loudly to convey that I'd rather spend a sunny Saturday in someone else's company. As if possessed, the tiny woman falls on the lemons like a dervish and begins pelting me. When she stops, the brown bag is empty, my back is to the wall, and we are both crying.

Afterward, we go on as if nothing has happened. I hold

out my hands for her to inspect them; dirty or not, she sends me to wash them, and then we sit side by side and creep through the Gospels. Both of us follow her finger, which pulls up short at each miracle, like a car at a scenic stop, so we can step out of the text to gawk. I don't care about water changing to wine or multiplying fishes, only about miracles that teeter dizzily, like Jesus himself, between this life and another, as when he retrieves Jairus's daughter from the dream that stole her away or raises Lazarus from the dead. That he healed lepers, paralytics, and the woman with the "issue of blood" suggests that illness does exist, but that is nothing as confounding as his resurrected body.

"Reach out your hand and put it into my side," Jesus says to his apostle Thomas, for whom it isn't enough to see what the blood of the risen Christ might be.

Like stained glass, I think. Red that isn't blood but light. Red that splatters on the floor and red we are to drink.

"Where did it come from?" I ask Libby about the affliction of the woman who bled for twelve years before Jesus touched her.

"Does it make a difference?"

"I just want to know."

Libby lifts her shoulders, narrower than my own. "It doesn't say," she says. I suspect she knows the answer and is withholding it from me.

"Did he die coughing up blood?" I ask my grandfather about his father.

"I suppose he must have." My grandfather has given up trying to dilute the sick awe that blood summons in me. Although he does confiscate the stereoscope cards of the Boxer Rebellion, with decapitated bodies next to their heads, blood spilled all over like pools of black ink.

S.S.B. ON LUGGAGE, on dishes, on monogrammed linens, on the cover of his Remington "Noiseless" typewriter, etched into the back of his pocket watch, pressed into the disk of gold set into the ivory head of his walking stick, like a coin, a private currency. S.S.B. Engraved on solid sterling serving trays, punch bowls, baby rattles, a gold cigar case and lighter. Solomon Sassoon Benjamin is everywhere in our house, holding what's left of us together, as all the money we have, all that is draining away, is money he made in China in the nineteenth century.

It will be decades before I discover, from an epitaph in Hong Kong's Jewish cemetery, how Solomon Sassoon Benjamin's first marriage ended, words writ, like a commandment, in stone: *Sacred to the memory of Fanny the dearly beloved wife of S. S. Benjamin, born in London, 23 August 1867, died Monday, 8 July 1892, Gone in Life's Bright Morn, Gone in Her Youthful Bloom.* Fanny was twenty-five and died in childbirth. The epitaph next to hers is for Claude, who followed her on November 11, 1892. *Infant Son of S. S. Benjamin, aged Four months and three days.*

The monument, an obelisk, occupies the most desirable block of the eastern end of the necropolis. The view is better from the east, and the real estate expensive, a gated community overlooking Repulse Bay. Baghdadi Jews had lived in Hong Kong for centuries before the first wave of Ashkenazi refugees washed ashore and found themselves in the servant class, waiting tables, washing linens, scrubbing floors. When they died, they were buried downhill, where plots were narrow and there wasn't any view. It is an arrangement my grandmother would have approved.

A marble plaque, dated 1855, dedicates the cemetery to the man who proved himself the British Empire's djinn from a bottle. The plaque, like the rest of the cemetery, is invisible from the street:

> For the souls who have departed this life for their Master in the holy community of Hong Kong, may G-d protect it. And this land is a gift of our mistress the Queen (Victoria), may G-d bless her, given with payment in full a sum of money that was necessary by David Sassoon in the year 1855, may he see offspring and have a long life.

So it happened twice that my great-grandfather lost his little boy, both firstborn and last: my grandmother's baby brother died eleven years later, when he was not a year old and she was just four.

It happened twice, and the second time Solomon Sassoon Benjamin had a nervous breakdown. "I saw him from the corridor," my grandmother tells me. "He was in his dressing room, and he was holding on to the drapes, or a chair—he dragged something down onto the floor with him—and I was frightened of the noise he was making. He prostrated himself and he didn't get up. He stayed there on the floor. Someone—the amah, I suppose—took me away." My grandmother tells me something else frightened her too: she'd been jealous of the baby, she'd wished him ill, and she admits it, she still feels bad.

"What does *prostrated* mean?"

"That he fell on his face on the ground." She heard what she'd never heard before, she tells me: she heard her father crying. Maybe this is when, or maybe it's how, my grandmother fell in love with her father; maybe it's why she never grows out of it. The shock of witnessing a thing so terrible, a thing that could fell her father and like a great boot grind him into the floor. And then, having seen such a thing, the determination to redeem a thought so wicked.

"You didn't kill him," I say.

"I pinched him, though. I made him cry. I may have wished he was dead."

"You were only four," I say from the august vantage of nine. "You probably didn't know what dead means."

"Everyone knows what dead means."

I can tell by the way my grandmother speaks of her father, with affection she doesn't waste on past lovers, that thirty years after his death he hasn't faded, he's more real to her than a lot of living people. For all my life I will think of Solomon Sassoon Benjamin's grief before I do his illustrious family, before his millions, made and lost and made again, a fortune my spendthrift mother will do her best to squander, perhaps suffering a presentiment that, just as motherhood came too early, so premature death would cheat her of her inheritance.

For all my life when I think of my great-grandfather, I won't see the man from my grandmother's photograph albums: impeccably dressed with his gold watch and fobs, the Homburg hat incongruous over his brown face. His skin was dark enough to bring him prejudice rather than success in London and sent him back to the Orient to make his fortunes. That picture won't be the first that comes to the mind of Solomon Sassoon Benjamin's only great-grandchild. I will always remember him as a man begging, facedown, for the life of his son to be returned.

"He had two nervous breakdowns," my grandfather says. "He was a stockbroker—well, futures, really—and made quite a fortune and then lost the whole thing in—"

"Futures?"

"It's a man who speculates, who sells—well, in this case it was India rubber, tapped from rubber trees—"

"Like maple syrup?"

"Not syrup, sap. Maybe millions of shares in the rubber market, and the bottom fell out of the market. Half of the bankers in—"

"How can a market's bottom fall out?" This makes no sense.

"It's an expression. It means the value of shares goes down suddenly—"

"Shares?"

"Listen, will you? In this case the new automobile industry, it's 1910, remember, which was growing very fast, predicted a great need for rubber tires—"

"It's okay," I say, sensing a mathematical trend, "you don't have to tell me that part."

"What it boiled down to was half the brokers in Shanghai went bankrupt—it wasn't only your great-grandfather who lost everything. They were—the whole family was on holiday in England when they learned of the crash, and then . . ."

"And then what?"

"Then he had a nervous breakdown and was in a sanitarium in the South of France. Where the family returned after they left the Orient."

"I thought sanitariums were for consumption."

"Not all of them."

"What is a nervous breakdown?" There have been several, I know, in my grandmother's family, whose strings are tightly strung.

"It's what happens when a person can't go on as usual, because he's too shocked, something terrible has happened, or there has been too much strain for too long, that kind of thing."

"So what happens to them?"

"They rest until they are better. Your great-grandfather did go back to Shanghai," he says, "and he paid every debt, and recouped some part of his fortune."

"What was the baby's name?"

"Whose baby?"

"Nana's little brother who died."

"I don't remember—I'm not sure I ever knew. Ask her, why don't you?"

"Everyone had the same names," she tells me. "That's why my father's father turned his surnames around, from Benjamin Sassoon to Sassoon Benjamin, so as not to get mixed up with a cousin."

"But what was the baby's name?"

"David."

"After Sheik David?"

"There's a David on every twig," she says of the family tree, and she tells me the story of the bris that didn't happen, because when my great-grandmother saw the crescent of dirt under the Shanghai mohel's long thumbnail, filed sharp to slice off baby boys' foreskins, she lunged forward, snatched her little boy away, right off the pillow and out of reach of the mohel. They'd wait and have it done the next time they were in London.

But before they made their yearly pilgrimage to Europe, David had died, uncircumcised. A teething infection went to his brain and killed him. A punishment from God, according to the Orthodox community, who learned what had happened at the bris, but to his family's mind, he died of China. From this point forward, the family's level of vigilance against germs reached a point of hysteria. Shanghai's filth was not confined to the underside of the mohel's thumbnail. What amount of money could contain or beat it back? What amount could protect them?

There's an epilogue to David's death; my grandmother never leaves it out.

"My parents had a cherub on the headstone, a marble one sitting on top, and as that sort of thing wasn't tolerated by the frum who—"

"What's a frum?"

"Orthodox. Aside from the little angel, it was against Orthodox law to bury an uncircumcised baby in their *hallowed ground*." She spits the words. "So someone came in the night and smashed the stone to bits." She doesn't have to tell me what she believes. If a sacrilege was committed, it was by whoever was wicked enough to heap more misery on a bereaved family.

School of Fragonard, pastel.

FOR THE LAST few weeks of fourth grade I'm popular. I don't have to ask classmates over; they invite themselves. I wait a day and then tell whoever it is that my grandparents said no.

"She dared them," Francesca says about the girl with the black bob, the one who dropped her satchel and covered her ears even before all the unsynchronized clocks began striking. We're in the back of a station wagon, carpooling home from a birthday party.

"What do you mean, dared?" I ask.

Francesca is the only child I know whose family mirrors mine—absent father and flighty young mother who left her in the care of her ancient Old World parents. The best thing about Francesca is that she doesn't ask questions I can't answer.

"To go over to your house, stupid." She takes a happy-face button off her sweater, bends the pin out from behind it, and starts poking its point through the vinyl-upholstered seat, making a little line of holes. "She told everyone it made sense you were such a weirdo," she says of the black-haired girl, who hated the food in our pantry even more than the clocks in the living room. "Peek Frean? Peek Frean? What's a Peek Frean? Don't you have Oreos?" She was so desperate she sang the jingle that went with the commercial.

She'd also been astonished to find herself doing homework under supervision rather than playing or watching TV. When my grandfather said, as he always did when I was doing math, that I must take as much care to solve the last problem as I had the first, she made a face behind his back, and I answered it with one she didn't expect.

"Also she said your room was babyish and didn't even belong to you, there was another girl's name written all over, and everything in the house was creepy like *The Addams Family,* especially the empty places where the paintings used to be, and the one that's left was so creepy it made her scared about what the others were and where they went. She said you catch lizards and your grandfather is mean."

"One lizard! It was on the steps in front of the house!"

"So?"

So it was right there in front of me. I could not stay my hand.

I consider the white toy chest with the little lamb

painted on the front. There's a white rocking chair too. Both are from my mother's childhood bedroom; both bear her name, Carole, painted in pink. A lot of stuffed animals. Not only no Barbies but no dolls of any kind, as I hate them, especially the ones with eyes that fly open when you stand them up and most of all the babies that eat and drink and mess their diapers. Those I wouldn't touch. I've seen *The Addams Family,* so I know what it means when classmates call me Cousin It. I hate the painting that's left too, but not because its subject scares me. It was supposed to be a real Fragonard but turned out to be something called school of Fragonard, and not worth the trouble to sell. So there she hangs, with her flower basket and perfidious smile, helpless to help us.

"The books aren't for babies. Also, I have a lot of Legos and Hot Wheels."

"Hot Wheels are for boys."

I don't answer. Each time the pin goes through the vinyl it makes a little pop. Francesca likes breaking things. When she's inside our house, I keep her away from the sideboard, sitting smug in its recent appraisal, enough to forestall the inevitable for a few more months. Ever since my seventh birthday, when my room was overrun by guests for a party I didn't want, I've kept everything I care about upstairs in the library, out of sight. I have a Lionel train with a little brown glass bottle of liquid smoke and an eyedropper to place a single drop of it down the hot stack to make real plumes of smoke. Because I've laid out the track on an ancient carpet no one wants to buy, I can leave it there as long as I like. I didn't have to take the photographs upstairs; that's where I found them when I moved in, along with scrapbooks and condolence cards my grandmother received after the death of her father. There are letters, diaries, an ancient paper doll, and a party favor from New Year's Eve, 1917, when she was dressed as a Hawaiian. Edelweiss picked in 1925 and pressed between the pages of a Baedeker guide to Switzerland. Menus and stateroom plans saved from each of Cunard's great trio of ocean liners: the RMS *Mauretania,* the RMS *Lusitania,* and the RMS *Aquitania.*

Once, when Francesca's grandmother comes to pick her up, she doesn't hide at the sound of the doorbell but runs toward the foyer, where she kicks the tiny woman in the shins. I'd never think of doing such a thing to my grandmother—I wouldn't want to. Still, Francesca's insurgence thrills me. She bends the pin back, replaces the happy face over the monogram on her cardigan, and asks if I want to taste her tongue.

"Okay," I say, after considering the invitation.

"I'm right, aren't I?" she says of my unprecedented popularity being the result of a dare.

I shrug. "It's not like I wanted to be friends with any of them."

I walk up the driveway with the slippery taste of Francesca still on my tongue, slightly metallic. Even though I am not left-handed like my mother or Aunt Cecily, perhaps I have succumbed to lesbianism. I don't like boys, especially André, foisted upon me because he is the son of a distant cousin. He speaks only French and asks me to play doctor and pretends he doesn't understand when I say I don't want to, even if I say it in French.

I attend school, ballet lessons, birthday parties, but I live where I can't be followed, where I don't need and wouldn't bring other children, who are either heedless, like Francesca, or dismissive, like the black-haired girl. I'm the only one who goes upstairs to the dusty little library except for Mitzi, with her pink-padded paws and eyes the pale green of new grass. I lie on my back on the floor and she lies on my chest and we look at each other and sometimes she purrs and sometimes she doesn't, and I wonder if under her beautiful long coat she doesn't find my furless skin exceedingly ugly, the way I do the naked mole rat at the zoo.

The little window at the top of the stairs is made of leaded bottle bottoms. Up or down, I never pass it that I don't put my eye to each and look out at the garden. By now it is a superstition; a bad thing, I'm not sure what, will happen if I don't. A spell will break. Aquamarine, green, amber, mauve, sepia like the photographs, my avocado tree turned blue, the bright sky darkened: their concavity, convexity, irregularities on the glass, bend the little orchard, stretch my tree higher.

"Why is it?" I ask my grandfather.

"Why is what?"

"Why is it made out of bottle bottoms?"

"For the fun of it, that's all."

MY GRANDFATHER IS the only person who warns me that he will die someday and not be there, and that I would be fine. It's the one time in my life I know he's not telling the truth. He doesn't know he's lying, but I do.

He uses objects to tell me—ones I love, like the little man in the kayak, a single piece of scrimshaw placed in the curio cabinet among my grandmother's finely carved Chinese ivories, which are so detailed that a man three inches tall has teeth in his mouth, each smaller than a salt crystal, distinct from its neighbor.

My grandfather reaches behind the cabinet's glass door and puts the kayak on my palm.

A single Aleut, alone in his crude boat, with a hole through each round fist, one to fit a spear, the other for an oar, both of them lost. His body is a blob of parka, his head hidden by its hood. He's different from the ivories—I'm allowed to hold him, feel how much rougher the scrimshaw is than the velvety ivories, which I touch rarely and only under supervision.

"One day this will be yours," he says, and I tell him, every time, to please take it away, this thing I love, I don't want it.

"Please," I say, and he replaces the little man on the glass shelf.

The bottom of the cabinet is hidden from view and holds as many bowls of water as my grandmother can fit inside it. They're the same Pyrex bowls she uses for custards; they cycle through the kitchen and the curio cabinet. My grandfather has explained how ivory cracks without water vapor in the air.

"Will the little man in the boat crack?"

"He hasn't so far."

"He's made of whalebone."

"Yes."

The ivories vanish, one by one. They leave in order of descending value. I know this, but for me it's the opposite. Although I know the ivories have the power to keep foreclosure at bay, for me the one little Aleut in his boat is worth more than all the rest.

"What will happen when there's nothing left to sell? Will Nana call the trust officer?" I know of trusts and their officers, although I picture the officer with a policeman's hat and badge inscribed *Trust*. In fact I know more than I want to about money, as it is a frequent topic of loud argument.

My grandfather nods, but it's more of a thoughtful nod than an answer to the question.

The lamps with the colored glass shades, the three ship lanterns, the barometer with the moon and sun on its cheeks, the star sapphire ring that he slips from his little finger so I can hold it before the sun to see the stone flash. The photographs he took in Alaska. I can't hate any of these things, but already, in advance of his death, they speak of grief.

"You have a second heart," I tell my grandfather. "You said you do."

"It's an expression. Like 'eyes in the back of your head.' "

"No. You said your constitution was forged in Alaska and your legs are your second heart." My grandfather says nothing. "That is what you said," I say.

"TELL ME ABOUT Emile."

"Again? What do you want to hear about that for?"

"Tell me what happened. I like to hear you tell it." I know her protests are perfunctory; her favorite stories are of spurned suitors.

Each photograph of Emile-with-no-surname, as my grandmother claims she cannot remember it, predicts a humiliation he didn't expect. My grandmother is bored to the point of hostility. She sits beside him on the beach in Japan, smoldering, but not with passion for him. When I remember that it was Cecily on the other side of the camera's lens, I wonder if my grandmother isn't glaring at her sister.

My grandmother and Emile, Lake Hakone,
Japan, 1917.

"The dress was the worst of it," I begin for her, and she nods.

"The dress and the gifts." The dress was made to order in Paris, by Lanvin, and had a six-foot train. Along with my nineteen-year-old grandmother's entire trousseau, it was packed in layers of tissue paper and shipped to Shanghai.

"It was sold at an auction to benefit the fever hospital," she says. "Or maybe it was smallpox. Something dreadful." One couldn't, after all, return a couturier wedding gown. "The underclothes—those I kept." The lace on her lingerie had been made by Belgian nuns. Handwork of virgins, it trimmed knickers and negligées, brassieres, chemises, garter belts. Everything as white as cake icing, ready to be stripped away on the wedding night.

Gifts that arrive in advance of a wedding that doesn't take place have to be returned, of course, each with a letter of apology.

"What did you say?"

"That I was sorry, I suppose."

"You weren't, though."

"No."

"You were relieved."

"I was." She smiles.

"How many?"

"How many what?"

"How many men did you jilt?"

"Well, jilt, that means at the altar. Only one."

My grandmother marches out of the synagogue on Peking Road and turns left. How many minutes can it have taken to walk four blocks east to the Bund? On the way, her heavy hair spits out the pins and tumbles down her back, shines dark against the white dress. She glides like a float, feet invisible, past the Bund's intersection with Jinkee Road, where her father kept his brokerage: a victory parade along the most important road in all the world that was Shanghai. The wide boulevard separated a long queue of European banks from the Whangpoo, a flat silty snake of a river coiling sluggishly, sucking and dragging at its own muddy bed.

"Why was it yellow?"

"Because it was filthy."

Emile was the first and most spectacular failure of my great-grandfather's attempts to marry my grandmother to a safe man he knew personally, through business. He rewarded her for the catastrophe, spiriting her away from the gossiping International Settlement and off to California. The next time, and the one after that, she broke off engagements.

Lawrence Kadoorie and my grandmother at Lake Hakone, Japan, 1917.

"You didn't ever tell Lawrence you'd marry him."

"Not really, no."

"Even though he had all that money."

"Even though."

"Even though you'd known him all your life and liked him." Even though they had played together as children, to be shackled to her father's business partner was not a thing she would do.

"There's an expression," she says. " 'Familiarity breeds contempt.' "

"Also," I say, "the shirt cuff."

"The shirt cuff most of all." Because a long time ago, in Shanghai, when she and the future Lord Kadoorie were dining out, he added up the tab on the cuff of his shirt.

"Now tell me," she says, "how could I marry a man like that!"

IT'S RAINING WHEN my ransacking search for amusement takes me as far as my grandparents' bathroom drawers, one filled with new toothbrushes—my grandmother's preoccupation with germs demands that she change hers weekly—another with Q-tips and cotton balls and extra bars of soap, and a third with only my grandfather's black leather dopp kit, unused because we don't travel. We drive

to and from La Jolla, where we spend half of July and all of August in a cottage at the beach, the car "packed to the gunwales," according to my grandmother, "making us look like Okies," but then we are not so much traveling as changing households for a spell.

The kit smells like him, or his cologne, and a flat pocket holds a mirror about the size of a postcard, its silver frame tarnished. When I pull it out, I find there is a photograph on the other side, one to which I'll return. I take it carefully from under the glass, turn it over to find a name on the other side—"Rose." I sit on the edge of the bathtub and try to see behind its subject's solemn eyes. Her face fills the frame; I can see it as I can't when she's standing on the ice floe. It's a heart-shaped face, earnest and innocent, and immediately

Spring breakup,
Anchorage, 1917.

I know that if he weren't still in love with her, he wouldn't need to hide her photograph from my grandmother, whose jealousy makes little distinction between the living and the dead. And if she were not hidden, I wouldn't have to come back to her as I do, spurred not by jealousy—it's closer to fear, my finding a rival. She was there all along and I didn't know it.

She has a voice but never speaks; she uses it to sing. All that's left of her are two scrapbooks of Bible lessons cut from a newspaper, a handful of photographs, a few songs (for Rose, like my grandfather's sisters, sang professionally), and the two sons she gave my grandfather, both away at war in Germany when my mother was born.

In Alaska, my grandfather went on losing one job after another. The only one he kept was working for himself, trapping fur. In 1914 he was fired by the Alaska-Gastineau Mining Company for not being able to keep a hundred Russian miners' names straight. He'd been the timekeeper, but he couldn't keep track of the hours worked by scores of men who spoke no English and drank themselves into a stupor every night. "I had to drag them up out of the holes of the boat," he tells me, and he says they were so tough they drank horse liniment if they couldn't find anything better.

"Why were they in boat holes if they were miners?"

"Only place the company had to put them. It was right on the Gastineau Channel, and—

"Anyway, I still had the job keeping books for a guy who owned a little drugstore in town, and so I used to see this girl quite often, when she came into the store. Because just up Main Street, such as it was, she had a job in what

was actually not a music hall but a tent theater. They used
to—"

"What do you mean, tent?"

"If you'd let me finish. Anchorage didn't have a theater,
but we had moving pictures—silent, of course—projected
onto the inside of a big tent. And she used to sing, to enter-
tain them. I remember one song she used to sing, 'Pretty
Baby,' and I fell in love with her. Completely, oh boy."

There's an upright piano in the tent, and a movie flickering on canvas stirred by a breeze. But the movie is silent;
no one plays the piano, the dark is filled with her voice. The
dogs howl, the rivers break to pieces, mosquitoes whine and
dive at ears and eyes, the audience fidgets and coughs on
split log benches, but for him all there is is the one voice,
nothing else.

I know it's cold and damp and buggy. He's told me
that he met her in the drugstore, that he knew her father,
a fur broker based in Seattle, and that the two of them got
together to *schmooze*. But I ignore details that don't serve the
romance I've conceived around a hidden photograph and a
song sung in a tent. For me all there is is the one voice in
the dark.

MISS ROBESON'S ACADEMY for Young Ladies came with Miss Robeson's mother, Ma Robey, whose purpose it was to stymie the boarders' hunger. Around the long table she crept, gnarled and bent like a witch. In my mind she is represented by a pair of twisted hands holding tight to the sides of a tray bearing a single serving of what was usually bread pudding, which appeared at every dinner.

"Doorstops, we called them," my grandmother says. "Great heavy slabs, an occasional currant. I'd die of dyspepsia if I ate it today."

Ma Robey crept between the tables and asked who wanted a second helping, which all the girls did and none dared to ask for, as the offer was always followed by, "Miss Robeson hasn't had hers yet." My grandmother makes her Ma Robey face, pulling her mouth into a pucker as if with a drawstring, followed by Miss Robeson's, which uses strings to different effect, pulling up her eyebrows and pulling down the corners to her lips. Also Miss Robeson had a lorgnette, which made her tilt her nose at an arrogant angle.

"Ma Robey said it every time?"

"Every time."

"Why didn't they just cook more food?" I ask.

"Save money, I suppose. There's nothing more beastly than an English boarding school."

"Except Shanghai," I say.

"And English country-house parties," she says, because even in August the houses were beastly rotten cold, everything was damp, including the draperies, everyone was too stuck up for words, the ladies' maids and gentlemen's valets even more than their employers, and there were never enough men to go around, the war took so many, and nothing to do except hunt foxes, which she never did, as it was cruel—she could ride well enough. "If you want to spend a day huddled on a hearth with a shawl over your shoulders and an uncut novel in your lap, then a country-house party is for you."

"How old were you when you stopped going to boarding school?"

"Fifteen, more or less. Once the war was on, we were stuck in Shanghai."

In 1979, "in response to a request for material to be included in a book" about Shanghai Jewry, Lawrence Kadoorie, eighty years old, narrated the history of his family, including those points at which it had intersected with that of my grandmother and her family. (The writer was Rena Krasno, the book *Strangers Always: A Jewish Family in Wartime Shanghai,* published in 1992.) It is transcribed in the form of a deposition, each paragraph numbered, 1 through 60:

> 19. In 1914 my mother and father, together with Mr. and Mrs. S. S. Benjamin, came to Banff in Canada to spend the summer holidays with their children, who were arriving from school in England.

20. It was whilst my brother [Horace] and I were crossing
the Atlantic in the charge of our respective governesses
that war broke out with the result that we could not get
back to school. After a series of adventures, during which
our large party ran out of cash, we all managed to get
back to Shanghai where we spent the rest of the war years.

Lawrence never expounds on the adventures, and my
grandmother never speaks of being stranded on the way
home, but her first photograph album to document the war
years traces the journey home from Banff, a city she remembers for its having provided her the opportunity to flirt with
the Prince of Wales, who was vacationing there at the same
time as she and her family.

Edward VIII, Prince of Wales,
Banff, 1914.

Five years my grandmother's senior,
Edward VIII posed for a picture and
gave her his signature. She was three
months shy of fifteen and under the
watch of a governess; it was nothing
that could be called a dalliance, and yet
it left my grandmother with an indelible schoolgirl crush, strong enough that
in her seventies she remains affronted
by Edward's having given up the Crown
for Wallis Simpson, whom my grandmother calls "that person," going so far
as to share with me a rumor that Mrs.
Simpson was born neither a girl nor a
boy but both. I don't know what a "her-
maphrodite" is, but I do know there's
little point in trying to pursue another
of what must be my grandmother's

Lake Minnewanka, 1914. My great-grandmother is in the foreground, with her back to the camera.

imagined ailments, a side effect of her hypochondria. As if it weren't enough to live in fear of microbes that do exist, she is tormented by conditions that are too outlandish to be true. Too, she suffers remote jealousies and is genuinely miffed when my grandfather voices his appreciation for Julie Andrews.

Of diversions, other than royalty, my grandmother says little, but her photograph album, executed with her characteristic untidy haste, traces a slow journey west to China. From Banff, where they picnicked in splendid fashion at Lake Min-newanka, sitting on chairs at a table set with a white cloth, china, and silverware, they took the Canadian Pacific Railway to Victoria, from which the large and nearly bankrupt party sailed south on the *Princess Alice.* One photograph, captioned by my grandmother as "Our Wreck,"

A fire drill aboard the RMS Empress of Britain, *July 24, 1914.*

shows a small ship heading back to shore tugging a lifeboat filled with a party of passengers taken from the disabled *Alice.*

Eventually they alighted in San Francisco and remained in the Bay Area long enough to see the Panama-Pacific International Expo in the city, go horseback riding in San Jose, visit the rebuilt Stanford University campus, which the 1904 earthquake had reduced to rubble, and stay at the famed Del Monte in Monterey, where they explored the French Hotel, notable for having been Robert Louis Stevenson's home in 1879. It would be hard to overestimate Robert Louis Stevenson's international celebrity. Twenty years after his death, his former possessions had become relics, his homes shrines. The traveling party would follow his path across the Pacific.

From San Francisco, the Kadoories and the Sassoon Benjamins set sail west. For my grandmother, a fire drill is novel enough to claim a place, caption, and exclamation point.

They stopped in the "Sandwich Islands," where my grandmother bought a grass skirt and silk leis she'd use for a fancy-dress ball on New Year's Eve 1917, in Miyanoshita, Japan, her face tinted as dark as her father's.

Midway between the Sandwich Islands and Australia was Samoa, where they disembarked on the island of Apia to visit Stevenson's home in Upolu, where, in 1894, after a lifetime of ill health, he succumbed to what was assumed to be tuberculosis.

In Australia my grandmother's family paused in New South Wales to visit relatives. They spent a week in the Philippines, of which she speaks with fondness; paused in Hong Kong for another week, this one for business; then Shanghai. Which wasn't home, exactly.

They returned to what they and many others in the International Concession considered a temporary place of rest, parochial, pestilential, a trial to be borne. Families who lived years longer in China than they did in Europe did not call Shanghai "home." Baghdadis like my great-grandfather pointed themselves west rather than east and retired to

Upolu, Samoa, 1914. S.S.B., Elly Kadoorie, and my grandmother (in the black hat) to the right of her father; her and Lawrence's mother in the foreground. Cecily, wearing an outfit identical to my grandmother's, is fourth from the far right.

Europe. It had been evident for years that the Ottoman Empire would topple, as it did in 1922, the same year the Sassoon Benjamins moved into Villa Edgerton.

MY GRANDFATHER STANDS over his cracked leather armchair, waiting for me to get out of it.

"At the end of this chapter." I show him it's only a few pages.

"Bring it with you," he says.

Outside it's sunny, it's warm. I don't know why I am to bring a book where it can only get dirty. I follow him across the driveway and past the fishpond, through the fruit trees to the biggest of all, the immense avocado I consider my own, fifty feet tall, with boughs as thick around as my waist that drop all the way to the ground, so you don't walk under it so much as through its cloak of leaves, using your hands to part it before you, and then you are inside it, surrounded by a tent fifty feet high, with chips of blue sky blowing through the leaves. This tree is fey and fairy-dusted; a spell has set its limbs so they ascend around the huge trunk like the treads on a spiral staircase.

"Even an old man can walk up them," my grandfather says, and I tell him he isn't old, and he says that next year he'll be eighty. I follow his finger with my eyes and see he's built something into the highest sturdy branch.

"What is it?"

"Take a look," he says. "Go on," and I do, almost loping up and around the trunk. I've climbed it so often I can do it eyes shut.

"You forgot your book!" he calls when he sees I've reached it: a chair with arms but no legs, a back as straight as a pew's. When I stand on its seat my head breaks through the canopy. Far below me, the neighbor boys' treehouse is as good as earthbound, and my longing for its trap door and rope ladder evaporates. My grandfather has sanded the chair carefully, I see when I sit back down. I'll never get a splinter in the heel of my hand or the backs of my thighs.

"Why are you crying?" he asks when I am on the ground, my arms just long enough to reach around him, my right cheek pressed tight to his chest. "Don't you like it?" I pull away, nodding.

"I love it. I love it more than anything. More than my bicycle."

He holds out my book and I take it up the tree and then, having reconsidered, bring it back down.

"It's the wrong one," I explain, and I run back to my room.

"Why?" he asks again at bedtime, after the light is out and the right book—*Alice in Wonderland*—has been consumed in the tree, cover to cover—I've read it several times already, so it goes fast, but still I barely make it down by bathtime. I shake my head against the pillow. I find his hand in the dark and fit mine into it.

"My head goes through the top."

"Yes," he says, and he asks me what I saw.

"Everything," I say. "I saw the beach. I saw the Ferris wheel on the Santa Monica pier."

He laughs. "I don't think so," he says.

I know I did. And I tell him all the other things I saw too. The Farmers Market and the Griffith Observatory and the oozing La Brea Tar Pits. There wasn't a thing I didn't see.

UP COUNTRY, my grandmother titles her album of photographs from three excursions the Sassoon Benjamins made into China during 1915. As usual, they and the Kadoories vacationed together, this time occupying two houseboats, the *Zaida* and the *Sheldrek*—names that suggest the families rented the boats and engaged the boatmen through a trusted Jewish agent. On May 1 they left Shanghai for a five-day trip to Hangchow—Hangzhou—about 120 miles southwest of Shanghai. Hangzhou was easily accessible by train, as China had granted Britain the right

Lawrence, my grandmother, and her parents on board the Zaida, *Hangchow, May 1, 1915.*

to construct a railway between the two cities—an unusual, and controversial, concession made to a foreign nation, but the agreement favored Chinese enterprise. Hangzhou had long attracted Westerners, especially in the spring, when its gardens bloomed and West Lake was carpeted in pink lotus. Its trade was tourism—the families engaged guides to lead them from one relic to the next. Lingyin and Jingci temples, each filled with gongs and hung with banners; the Leifeng pagoda, within it the spirit of the White Snake that rose from the lake in hope of reaching immortality: They took in all the sights with genuine interest and, photographs reveal, a physical remove more common to African safaris. Perhaps a frisson of danger enhanced an exotic experience, one made as comfortable as possible by well-compensated English-speaking Chinese who served them in the manner of colonized servants. Souvenirs abounded. Hangzhou was an ideal place to buy—and sell—antiquities: ivories, cloisonné, porcelain, jade. All these and more traveled back to Europe with my grandmother's family.

Six months later the families made their second trip up-country, leaving for Soochow—Suzhou—on November 3. Sixty miles west of Shanghai, Suzhou was a shorter train ride, half the distance to Hangzhou.

Like Shanghai, Suzhou was in the Yangtze River delta and had been a cultural mecca for centuries, presenting yet more opportunities to be edified about Chinese architecture and traditions and to collect Ming vases. The families remained there until November 11. Six weeks later, on December 26, they embarked on a third and final trip up-country, back to Dahoo—Taihu—Lake, on whose eastern shore was Suzhou. For millennia the natural beauty of Taihu, round and ringed by scores of temples, classical gar-

My grandmother, far right in the front row, Soochow, December 1915.

dens, and pagodas, had drawn classical Chinese painters, who left more bounty.

The Sassoon Benjamins bought what their money could buy, museum-quality plunder that would circumnavigate the globe and come to rest in Los Angeles to pay property taxes, afford a new water heater and my exorbitant tuition bills, and then at last buckle, like the closet shelf under the weight of my mother's shoes.

"Why aren't there any pictures of Shanghai itself? You took pictures everywhere else."

"Why should I take pictures of a place I didn't want to remember?"

"But you took pictures when you went up-country."

"Oh, Hangchow, Soochow—those are beautiful places."

"There never was and never will be another city like Shanghai," Lawrence Kadoorie said, continuing his family's history. His account of his family's life is less personal than

it might be were he dictating his memoirs rather than pro-
viding information for another writer's book.

> 21. . . . a city of extreme contrasts, combining the
> attributes of both East and West. The Paris of the
> Orient, with its good and its bad, providing a paradise
> for adventurers. Here my brother and I continued our
> education—the international environment provided
> by Shanghai broadening our outlook and giving us an
> understanding of what it was to become a citizen of the
> world.

Whereas my grandmother's impressions of the city
are riddled with fear and loathing, Lawrence Kadoorie's
are filled with passion and affection. To be fair, his adventures were not of a picaresque nature; they were sanitized,
germ-free; they didn't even require him to go outdoors:
they were financial. The war years were boom years for
the treaty port, which gathered in whoever cared to enter,
requiring no proof of any citizenship. Organized crime,
not elected officials, governed the city, controlling labor as
well as goods. The city had an endless appetite for sailors,
stevedores, factory workers. The International Settlement
had an unslakable thirst for Western goods, commerce
being the sole connection they had with Europe, the very
same connection my grandmother still pursues. Liberty of
London. Fortnum & Mason. Twinings. Pears soap. Cuti-
cura. They were all mad for German cameras, and so they
had them.

Somerset Maugham's *Of Human Bondage;* gramophone
records; *The Old Huntsman,* a collection of poems by Siegfried
Sassoon; *Dubliners* by James Joyce; Conrad's *Heart of Dark-*

ness. And, of course, Stevenson's *Treasure Island, Kidnapped, The New Arabian Nights,* and *Strange Case of Dr Jekyll and Mr Hyde.* First editions, published in London, purchased and read in Shanghai, and then shipped back to Europe.

Between the world wars Shanghai's population doubled and then tripled. It was always consumed by what it loved best, the making of money—a city bent on diversion when it wasn't making money to pay for diversions. Parties were wilder, morals looser, opium plentiful. The nightlife was cosmopolitan but, unless one had the means to bribe or elude a chaperone, largely out of reach. Mahjong seized hold of the International Settlement. Sing-song girls walked down the street in broad daylight.

Cecily learned to play the piano; my grandmother taught herself to knit and race cars.

Cecily, on the left, and my grandmother, both camera-mad in Kyoto, 1916.

ONCE AGAIN SHE cried bitterly. My grandfather's brother, who signed up as soon as war was declared, had been wounded twice, once nearly fatally, and their mother pleaded with my grandfather to stay out of it, letter after letter. One son was enough, she said. She didn't know why Sid had jumped at the opportunity to go to war, but my grandfather did. His brother, the adventurer, had just been dishonorably discharged from the Mounties.

"Royal Canadian Mounted Police," I say, because I like the full name better than *Mounties*.

"Yes. So this is what happened. He met a girl off his beat—he had sixty square miles of beat to cover on horse, and he had a little cabin and a little stockade alongside in case a guy was unruly and he had to lock him up in it, so that was his beat, sixty square miles in Saskatchewan, right near the Alberta border."

Spell it, I say, and he does. S-A-S-K-A-T-C-H-E-W-A-N.

"So he was making his rounds one day and he met a girl on a farm, a little off his beat, and, well, one day the inspector came trooping by with all his retinue—"

"What's a retinue?"

"—no Sergeant Jacobs on the job. He was with this girl-friend of his. So they marched him off and put him in jail for six weeks. And as soon as he got out, he enlisted."

"What's a retinue?"

"A group, a bunch of guys."

"How many?"

"Oh, six or so."

By the time my grandfather followed Sid to France, his brother had been there for three years, the first Canadian wounded. "He was one of only twenty-one left out of his regiment!" My grandfather cannot say this too many times. He rarely speaks of his brother without adding what sounds like his epitaph, even if it is a testimony to his survival against all odds.

"How many is a regiment?"

"In this case, eleven hundred people."

"I can't be a slacker," my grandfather wrote to his mother from Anchorage. "I've got to do my job, with all these guys getting killed. I can't stay out of this."

The German Spring Offensive campaign began on March 21, 1918. A week later, on March 28, my grandfather enlisted in Vancouver, British Columbia. As a skilled railway employee, he was classified A2: someone whose engineering aptitude and employment history with the AEC would prove useful behind lines.

He tells me he was something called a sapper and that the word is from the French *saper*—to dig the foundation out from under something so it collapses.

Sapper, grenade, guerrilla, sabotage, bombardment, espionage. Revolver. Surrender. Armaments. Armistice. The words of warfare: so many are French, just like those my mother and grandmother use. *Tais-toi, tais-toi, tais-toi.* Shut up, shut up, shut up.

"We had to dynamite railway tracks, bridges—we were

SKILLED RAILWAY EMPLOYEES _Original_

Ex, B-C.R.M, U.S.A

ATTESTATION PAPER.

No. 2204754

Folio.

CANADIAN OVER-SEAS EXPEDITIONARY FORCE.

QUESTIONS TO BE PUT BEFORE ATTESTATION.

(ANSWERS)

1. What is your surname?		JACOBS.
1a. What are your Christian names?		HARRY SAMUEL.
1b. What is your present address?		Camp 4 Twohy Bros,Youngs Falls,Oregon,USA
2. In what Town, Township or Parish, and in what Country were you born?		London England.
3. What is the name of your next-of-kin?		Mrs Ø Lilian,Davis.
4. What is the address of your next-of-kin?		c/O Mrs Wood,The Green,Gringley-on-the-Hil Doncaster,Yorkshire,England. SUFFICIENT ADDRESS
4a. What is the relationship of your next-of-kin?		Mother.
5. What is the date of your birth?		July 29th 1890.
6. What is your Trade or Calling?		Accountant.
7. Are you married?		No.
8. Are you willing to be vaccinated or re-vaccinated and inoculated?		Yes.
9. Do you now belong to the Active Militia?		No.
10. Have you ever served in any Military Force? If so, state particulars of former Service.		Royal Bucks Hussars,4yrs, 1907-10.
11. Do you understand the nature and terms of your engagement?		Yes.
12. Are you willing to be attested to serve in the CANADIAN OVER-SEAS EXPEDITIONARY FORCE?		Yes.
13. Have you ever been discharged from any Branch of His Majesty's Forces as medically unfit?		No.
14. If so, what was the nature of the disability?		..
15. Have you ever offered to serve in any Branch of His Majesty's Forces and been rejected?		No.
16. If so, what was the reason?		..

DECLARATION TO BE MADE BY MAN ON ATTESTATION.

I, Harry,Samuel,Jacobs, do solemnly declare that the above are answers made by me to the above questions and that they are true, and that I am willing to fulfil the engagements by me now made, and I hereby engage and agree to serve in the Canadian Over-Seas Expeditionary Force, and to be attached to any arm of the service therein, for the term of one year, or during the war now existing between Great Britain and Germany should that war last longer than one year, and for six months after the termination of that war provided His Majesty should so long require my services, or until legally discharged.

Date..................191. ....(Signature of Recruit)
.......(Signature of Witness)

OATH TO BE TAKEN BY MAN ON ATTESTATION.

I, Harry,Samuel,Jacobs, do make Oath, that I will be faithful and bear true Allegiance to His Majesty King George the Fifth, His Heirs and Successors, and that I will as in duty bound honestly and faithfully defend His Majesty, His Heirs and Successors, in Person, Crown and Dignity, against all enemies, and will observe and obey all orders of His Majesty, His Heirs and Successors, and of all the Generals and Officers set over me. So help me God.

Date..................191. ....(Signature of Recruit)
.......(Signature of Witness)

CERTIFICATE OF MAGISTRATE.

The Recruit above-named was cautioned by me that if he made any false answer to any of the above questions he would be liable to be punished as provided in the Army Act.

The above questions were then read to the Recruit in my presence.

I have taken care that he understands each question, and that his answer to each question has been duly entered as replied to, and the said Recruit has made and signed the declaration and taken the oath

before me, at VICTORIA, B.C. this..................day of..................191. .

.......(Signature of Justice)

ATTESTING OFFICER

way up at the front, probably about twelve miles behind the lines."

Knowing how much work had gone into them, I ask him if it didn't feel bad, going from building bridges to blowing them up.

It didn't, he says, because it had to be done and blowing things up is an art. It's not what it looks like in the movies, it isn't fireworks but the opposite: using as few sticks of dynamite as possible and knowing exactly where to place them so a bridge's span collapses with as little noise as possible—a stealthy detonation if he worked in the dark, and having lived for years in Alaska, my grandfather could do most things in the dark. The fuse hisses, the well-placed sticks explode; the bridge's piers buckle and swoon, then sink under the surface of the river below. An elegant collapse, as if in slow motion, hardly a splash, the reflection of the moon on the water's surface breaking apart into bright chips.

On April 19 he was in Ontario, at the railway construction depot in Hamilton, having been whisked eastward in less than two weeks, thousands of miles and years of travel backtracked in what seemed like minutes. With orders to join the 6th Field Company of Royal Canadian Engineers, he was sent by train to Niagara Falls, for "gas-mask drills and that sort of thing," and from Niagara Falls on to England on the S.S. *Waimana,* and then, finally, he was at the front, reassigned to the 5th Battalion Construction Railway Troops. By the time he joined his unit in Annappes, near Lille, it was October—six months since he'd enlisted and, as it turned out, only a little over a month before the war ended.

My grandfather doesn't tell his own war stories, as there aren't any, really. The enemy line extended from Armen-

tières, on the Belgium border, about fifteen miles south to
La Bassée. Behind it, sappers prevented the movement of
German supplies and enabled the passage of Allied ones.
The field company's daily war diaries detail their every
Sisyphean chore as they built some things and took apart
others. There is the "reboring of bolt holes" and the "loading
and unloading of sand." The unit "collected scattered material into large dumps," recycled bombed track, salvaged old
steel and cut it into lengths. They "removed" a bridge "to
allow barges to pass." The single incident of interest was the
discovery, on November 7, 1918, "of 5 delay action mines"
in the Ascq train yard. Subsequent weeks are devoted to the
discovery and extraction of other land mines. A successful
undertaking: no one was injured.

As he hasn't any of his own, my grandfather tells me
about his brother's war stories and injuries. The only thing
that saved Sid, he says, was that he was blasted out of the
trench onto the parapet. But he'd been chlorine gassed—

"What's a parapet?"

"It's a—well, it's a low wall just before the trench, to
crouch behind and not get shot. So they brought him back
to England, and they brought my mother to see him because
they didn't think they could save him, he was green all over,
from the gas."

"What do you mean, green all over?"

"I mean green. Anyway, I told her I couldn't stay out of
it any longer."

ON THE OTHER side of the world, the Sassoon Benjamins had seen all of China they cared to, from the squalid to the picturesque. Until the war was over and they could travel further afield, they spent as many months a year in Japan as Benjamin, Kelly, and Potts could spare Uncle Dick—as his wife, Dollie, intended, no one called him Solomon. They traveled with the Kadoories sometimes, and sometimes with my grandmother's cousins, Albert and Ellis Hayim, her father's sister Hanini's sons. Albert and Ellis made the same pilgrimage to Shanghai as my great-grandfather had twenty years before them, from Baghdad to Bombay (where they, like he, became British subjects) and on to Sydney, Hong Kong, and finally Shanghai, where they began an apprenticeship that would end in Albert's making more money than Benjamin, Kelly, and Potts's fortunes combined, inspiring my great-grandfather's pride, not envy. Having lost two sons, Uncle Dick found unexpected comfort in his nephews, especially extroverted Albert, who was a tease like himself.

Albert Hayim, Baghdad.

My grandmother's albums from Japan suggest that the Sassoon Benjamins were the hearty sporting family they were not. But they did consider Japan's climate and hygiene the antidote to spending most of the year in an atmosphere considered especially hazardous to children—one motivation for sending my grandmother and her sister to a boarding school nearly six thousand miles away.

The Solomon Benjamins didn't talk about the little boy they had lost, but he couldn't be banished. A determined little ghost, trapped in time and underfoot, he creeps after the family out of one photo album and on into the next, trying to catch hold of his father's trouser cuff. At first you don't see him. Then, once you've looked at his father's eyes, you can't get rid of him. He has become the expression on my great-grandfather's face. Not that his mother didn't grieve, but she never looks directly at the camera. She believed he would have lived had they been in London when his molar broke through and opened his mouth to infection; this has become a family myth, incontrovertible. To challenge it is to somehow diminish the family's suffering, as if it would be less agonizing to have lost a child in London, where they could have afforded the best medical attention to be had. As it was, wherever he fell ill, no amount of money could have saved him; there were no antibiotics in 1903. But, the myth insists, none would have been needed, as London was clean, not saturated with filthy foreign microbes.

In reality, London's East End was as overcrowded and in want of plumbing as a Chinese slum, and the city endured outbreaks of diseases, such as cholera, that presented little threat to the affluent inhabitants of the International Settlement.

.   .   .

Sixty, seventy years later, in a restaurant my grandmother patronizes routinely, she dissects her food before
taking a bite. She cannot stop herself from lifting the crust
off a potpie to fish around its filling for I'm not sure what.

"If it's a germ, you can't find it with a fork, Nana." I say
it more than once, but she never answers; she goes on taking
apart a sandwich and peering at its every element before reas-
sembling it. Unwraps a teabag so carefully a stranger would
think she expected to find its original content replaced by a
sachet of contagion.

China was pestilential, but in Japan the Sassoon Benjamins and their traveling companions bathed in the sea,
soaked in hot springs, toured the countryside in an open
car, and tried to find as many of Hokusai's thirty-six views
of Mount Fuji as they could. They hiked
where it was possible, picnicked outdoors.
My great-grandfather posed with a racket
and perhaps even played tennis.

They stayed in hotels that had long
catered to aristocracy, even royalty. Queen
Victoria entrusted Prince Albert to the care
of the Fujiya in Miyanoshita; the Prince of
Wales stayed at the Lakeside Hotel, on the
shore of Lake Chuzenji. The fantastically
shaped group of islands known as Matsu-
shima had the Park Hotel, whose guests were
interchangeable with those at the Fujiya. The
same people, or people like them, were waiting in Kyoto, at the Sakamoto, often taking
the same day trip on the same day.

Within the safe embrace of such estab-
lishments, my grandmother's mother could

be persuaded to go outdoors; she didn't worry about germs on doorknobs or using a water closet that might prove fatal. Summers, the family avoided the worst of Shanghai's pestilential swelter, not to mention the smell. Winter was serene; there was snow: clean, white, and silent.

The photographs my grandmother took in Japan are different from those glued into her "Up Country" album, which are far fewer and have a comparatively perfunctory quality when compared to the ones taken in Japan. My grandmother is now a more seasoned photographer, but it's not that, or not that alone. The eye behind the lens likes what it sees. What it sees summons artistry, even love. Some of the prints are hand-tinted, cherry blossoms washed pink, pale lips made red.

Nikko's ornate shrine, as technicolored as Red Square's onion domes; Kyoto's Golden Pavilion; Nara's sacred deer: the family hired educated guides. A stream of chaperones accompanied the sisters on jaunts that didn't include their parents: Mrs. Smeaton, Miss Herrer, Mrs. Armstrong, none of whom paid attention to my grandmother, as they were consumed by her sister and she by them.

Cecily on the bridge, Miyanoshita, 1919.

Snowscape, Miyanoshita, 1919.   *Kawoki Lane, Miyanoshita, 1919.*

Christmas Eve ball, Fujiya Hotel, Miyanoshita, 1919. My grandmother is in the second row, fifth from the left, and Cecily is eighth from the left.

"ZEISS," HE SAYS each time he pulls his binoculars from the red-velvet-lined case.

"Zeiss," I say back.

Zeiss makes the best lenses in the world. I wait until after he's dropped the strap around his neck before walking toward the water. He doesn't trust one lifeguard to keep watch over so many children.

We don't go to the beach so much as we move in for a day, carrying a room's worth of furnishings, enough to require several trips back and forth from the car's trunk to the sand. An umbrella of Brobdingnagian proportions provides enough shade to cover both card table and chairs and a wicker hamper too big to claim space on top of the table, as it is filled with plates and cutlery, napkins, salt and pepper shakers, radio, newspaper, magazines, zinc oxide to apply in broad stripes over my nose and under my eyes (my grandfather calls it war paint but fails to make me hate it less); a change of clothes for each of us hangs from the umbrella spokes above. Taken all together, it's more than my grandfather ever owned at one time when he was in Alaska; my grandmother's commitment to so outsized an undertaking the vestigial habit of someone who once could depend on limitless arms to do her bidding.

After lunch and behind her sunglasses, my grandmother is occupied by a favorite pastime: staring at other people.

Her gaze is strangely fixed on obese women, who are interesting dressed in street clothes and fascinating when in bathing costumes.

Omar the Tentmaker! she cries at first sight of a person so big she must be dressed in a tent. *Omar the Tentmaker!* Once, in the attempt to follow the trajectory of a great wobbling mountain of a person, she goes over backward in her beach chair.

None of us understands what my mother calls another of my grandmother's *idées fixes.* Five feet, two inches, she weighs far less than she would like. Croissants bearing slabs of butter, Black Forest cake, Lindt chocolate, eggs Benedict—each meal underscores her commitment to weigh as much as she can. At breakfast she pours heavy cream over dry cereal. But nothing works, because nothing can work. And the older and thinner she grows, the more firmly her obsession with fat women takes hold, developing a mathematical aspect as she discovers the pleasure of multiplying herself into their clothing. "Would you look at that! I could fit three of me into each leg of her trousers!"

My grandmother makes the kind of personal comments I have been taught never to say aloud. She gets away with it by using words like *sporran,* the furry pouch a Scotsman carries on a belt around his kilt, in lieu of *pubic hair.* American children are immigrants from *Bratislava. Bad tinkee* for *crazy* is borrowed from pidgin, like *No wanchee,* an acceptable response to the offer of a second helping. *No likee, no wanchee!* a more vehement rejection. How can it not be acceptable if she uses it herself? The best words are like *halem,* whose etymology is a story.

"The Halems were a family of Jews from Baghdad who moved to the International Settlement. They changed their name from Halem to Bottomly, and so my father—"

"Why would anyone do that?"

"Do what?"

"Change your name when you move."

"To sound British instead of Jewish."

"Bottomly sounds more like a name to get rid of than Halem," I say. I want to know why a person wouldn't want to sound Jewish, but I know it's the kind of question to save for my grandfather.

"Well, that's what they picked, and there you have it."

She uses *halem* when my grandfather says *backside* or *tuchus.*

The Halem Department! is a call to arms: what my grandmother cries when she sees the object of her fascination. "To the right, to the right! To the left!" If we don't look immediately, she directs our attention to what she's following behind her dark glasses.

"Keep your hair on," my grandfather says. He never looks up from what he's reading; she is too engrossed to notice.

MY GRANDFATHER REMAINED in France until January 23, 1919. Although it was announced that all rail work would cease on January 1, the 5th Battalion carried on as usual for another ten days, piling scrap, loading, unloading, and then, when they were finally released from duty, found themselves idly waiting for another two weeks for transport back to England.

"I was discharged in London in April, even though I was in the Canadian Army—that was a bit of a surprise. So I stayed with my mother, and she had a friend who was a manufacturer of sportswear, caps and so forth, up in Manchester. Another made topcoats, greatcoats, in London."

At his mother's urging, my grandfather went to see cousins living in Manchester. "Twelve of them, mind you," he tells me.

"Twelve cousins? Twelve children in one family?" From the point of view of an only child living with elderly grandparents, the five children next door present a pandemonium that's thrilling for a few hours and then, abruptly, unendurable. "The hooligans," my grandmother calls them, in this case a fair judgment. Their father is an absent airline pilot; their ex-stewardess mother begins drinking at breakfast; they have become feral. They use their bushes as toilets and run up trees naked. Their treehouse is for "booty"—what they steal from the family house to sell back to their mother.

Silverware and soap, mostly. I keep their secrets because tat-tling is dishonorable, and I don't want to lose permission to go over the fence for games my grandparents could never imagine me playing.

We each get a metal trash-can lid as a shield and what-ever piece of wood we can find as a weapon, and then there're no sides, just a melee as we each try to hit as many of the others as we can as hard as possible, except not above the neck and not anyone's privates. Bobby, Warren, and the baby don't present a problem, especially Bobby, who sucks on his two middle fingers and keeps his index and littlest finger shoved in his nostrils. With only one free hand he chooses a shield over a sword, but he's too listless, perhaps under-oxygenated, to be an obstacle to my sallies on his brothers. David is a year older than I and Greg a year younger, and they inflict injuries on my person, wounds I seethe to redress, so I hide what bruises I can lest I am denied the chance to come back a victor. Mostly I'm Joan of Arc, but as they don't know who she is, they can't agree to be the English. Which doesn't matter really, as it's easy to pretend they can't speak a language I understand; it's halfway true already.

Finally a split lip and a loosened tooth, which Tina (who happens to be working that day) reports to my grandmother when she returns from lunch out, result in a punitive cease-fire and the seizure of the trash-can lids. I can hear Tina shrieking in the foyer from where I sit in the bathtub, at five o'clock on the dot, loose tooth or not. My grandfather is paying a visit next door.

"*Petits cochons! Terrible. La mère est . . . est . . . La mère est impossible! Elle est inapte! Petit cochons! Dégoûtant! Madame—je—ah! Je ne sais pas. PETITS COCHONS!*" Little pigs.

It's a month before I'm allowed back over the fence,

having begged and wheedled until my grandparents' resistance breaks down. Greg has already forgotten my split lip. First he looks confused at my expression, then he gets up from where he was crouched on the grass and starts to run. Around and around his house—his legs are longer, but my rage is more tenacious than his fear, and even though he's bigger, he flags after the fourth lap. I come up from behind and trip him so he falls forward, hard enough to knock the breath out of him, and then I am on his back and pummeling him in an ecstasy of bloodlust, shocked by how good it feels to beat my fists on his sweaty back. David has to drag me off, pull the neck of Greg's T-shirt out of my clenched hand.

I wonder at myself, afterward, wonder at the raging girl I became, this me I'd yet to meet. Too young to understand that anger can misfire and hit a bystander, too frightened of what sets my mother and grandmother at each other's throats; all I know is the deep delight of satisfying it and the unease inspired by my discovery that I have a talent for hooliganism.

"Twelve cousins?" I ask my grandfather again. How can there be twelve when five is legion?

"Twelve," he confirms. "I asked one of them to take me to this friend of his and my mother's. I explained I was going back to the United States and asked if he was interested in selling his merchandise in the United States. He told me they'd never sold anything in America before, and I said he'd sell tons of it over there—see, they were hungry for British goods, they'd been shut off for four years. Sure enough, I got him to write me up an agreement giving me exclusive agency for the United States at ten percent commission.

"I was a good talker," my grandfather says. "I talked myself into another agency there. Beautiful topcoats, and rainproof wear for the upper crust—society people."

"People like Nana."

"People like Nana. So there I was, with a showroom just off Fifth Avenue in New York! Beautiful topcoats, all these samples, and I'd brought a lot more with me. The war had been over for maybe six months, and of course all these big department stores were hungry for British merchandise.

"I called on Saks! I called on Gimbels! Macy's! Everywhere I went they gave me huge orders! Gimbels! They asked me to bring my samples to his office in Philadelphia. Mr. Wana—it was Wanamaker—Mr. Wanamaker Jr. himself! I had a huge, double-door folding trunk with all my samples—an enormous thing—so they met me at the depot. They had a truck there and took my samples right back to his office, and there I was with the merchandise manager, the buyer, and Mr. Wanamaker."

It's a story my grandfather tells with wonderment, but the idea of chatting with Mr. Wanamaker wasn't enough to hold him in New York, a city he hated. Within eighteen months he was driving west to Los Angeles, with a pregnant wife in the passenger seat and a sample case behind them.

He never complains of the cold in Alaska. But winters in New York offended him in their dirtiness, the snow fouled by urine, horse dung, soot. The crowded streets and the clamor. For him, New York was another iteration of the landscape of his boyhood that he'd worked to escape. When he moved to Los Angeles he bought a plot "on Citrus Avenue, just off Wilshire Boulevard." He paid "three thousand dollars for the lot," cash. And he got "five percent off the cost of the house if I paid five percent cash down."

As far as he understood it, he'd "made a good deal—the house and lot all together cost about seven thousand. The house got built, we moved in there."

But by his own admission the good deal had landed them not on the periphery of the city but beyond its outskirts, "so far out that Wilshire Boulevard wasn't even paved between Western Avenue and La Brea. Unpaved, completely unpaved, so it was a terrible situation, because there was no place to shop—no place at all.

"I told my then brother-in-law, through marriage, in Los Angeles, that I'd had a house built for me way out, and he said, 'My God, you must have been out of your mind to build way out there, way out in the sticks.'"

WE RUN OUT of things to sell. The trust officer, with his badge that says *Trust,* grows deaf to my grandmother's pleas to invade the capital—this I see as resembling a statehouse under siege—and no longer sends her the mingy results of grudging invasions, not so much as a farthing, mind you. It's hard for me to gauge how dire our straits are, because my grandmother responds to routine bank statements as another person might react on being handed a death sentence.

She keeps careful accounts of small things, like money spent on stamps or buttons or tickets to the movies, adding columns of dollars and cents in the back of her little diaries. My grandfather has a proper desk, with a file drawer, and in it are tax documents and other things to which I am not privy and may not inquire about, as it is bad form for children to discuss any finances outside their weekly pin money, and then only behind closed doors, not in company.

At last it must be done. My grandmother writes a letter to her cousin, my Uncle Albert, who lives most of the year in Hong Kong. Without my great-grandfather, Albert might have nothing. Now he is both terribly rich and terrifically old. No one can count up his years or his money, no one but he, who visits every spring, and every spring speaks of my grandfather's jump on figures. Never in all his many years in finance has he seen anything remotely like it.

One spring, when we are having lunch with him at the

Beverly Wilshire Hotel, where he lives for his month in Los Angeles, he produces an astounding problem filled with horribly long numbers and pluses and minuses, and divisions and multiplications and percentages as well. He's written the problem down beforehand and has the correct answer written down as well.

My grandfather listens with his head slightly inclined to the right. About halfway through he closes his eyes and leaves them closed until Uncle Albert says the last number, and then he opens them and produces a string of numbers followed by a decimal point and a few more.

"Fantastic!" Albert says. He waves his long fingers in the air, and the waiter who stands by his table—his table, his waiter: like his valet, they are always the same—steps forward from his place on the periphery of our gathering to collect the basket of French rolls and bring them back so hot their toasted crusts crack open in his and my grandmother's hands. Each pulls out the doughy middle and passes it to me, as I like what they do not, and fills the shell with lumps of butter pressed into little flowers. Like my grandmother, Albert is very thin and dedicated to maintaining what weight he can.

As a young man in China, Albert made and wore a sandwich board that said "I AM THIN AND I KNOW IT." My grandmother wears an extraordinary number of undergarments, including a corsetlike girdle, to lend the appearance of heft under her clothes.

"Aren't girdles meant for fat people?" I ask as she steps into hers and pulls it up without any resistance.

"Gives me a little oomph," she says, and reminds me of the importance of standing up straight, especially when you get old.

"But you aren't old," I say as she steps into a full slip, a half slip, and another full.

I'm not sure how much money my grandmother asks him for. I imagine she named no figure, just said she was in bad straits.

It seems to me that a response late in coming will disappoint, but each day it doesn't appear, the check that will accompany it somehow gets larger, as if great hoops had to be cleared to effect so huge a gift.

My mother relaxes under the impression that suddenly money is about to be as it should: plentiful.

A PAPER DOLL, made by a friend in Japan. On the front is a portrait of my grandmother, on the verso farewell and best wishes, along with the expectation that my grandmother would return with her "husband of lawyer . . . I send this lovely style of yourself to you in good memory."

Like a letter, the paper doll is signed and dated—from Taka, on June 20, 1919.

"Don't forget!"

A "husband of lawyer"—what a preposterous idea, my

grandmother married to a lawyer, as preposterous as the idea that she would ever return to the Orient.

> 22. In 1919 our home in Shanghai caught fire and our mother [Laura Mocatta Kadoorie], a remarkable woman loved by all who knew her, lost her life by returning to the house to try to find the governess. It was after this that Horace and I took on a number of responsibilities formerly carried by our mother and did our share toward building up the Kadoorie name throughout Asia.

That was Lawrence's account. Cousin George remembers something else, calling it a "disgrace the way those two boys, eighteen and twenty, allowed their mother to go back into that house." George would have been an infant at the time, but it was common knowledge, he says, that they were the most dreadful and notorious cruel cowards, and that Lawrence and Horace lit horses' tails on fire for the fun of watching the animals bolt and, as they tried to outrun their agony, set other things alight.

"Now tell me, sweetie pie," George says, "if it weren't true, why would anybody be talking about it decades later?"

Laura, whom both boys resembled, was from an illustrious Sephardi family—a wealthy clan from Spain that transplanted themselves to Holland during the Inquisition. Long before Laura Mocatta married Elly Kadoorie, the Mocattas had moved again, to London, where in 1684 Mocatta & Goldsmid Ltd. became what it is today: silver broker to the Bank of England.

After the fire, Elly and his sons left Shanghai for London, where they remained for three years. In the meantime their home was being rebuilt to grandiose proportions.

25. . . . Unfortunately the architect, a Mr. Graham Brown, took to drink with the result that this residence became a palace. To put it mildly, it was something of a surprise to us, upon our return to Shanghai, to find the architect in hospital with the D.T.'s and a house with a ballroom 65' high, 80' long, and 50' wide, not to mention the other huge rooms, and a verandah 225' long.

It was never clear how much of the splendor had been commissioned. Once word arrived of the amount of marble the architect had shipped from Italy and its rumored cost, the Kadoories found themselves living in what neighbors called Marble Hall, a name that proved indelible.

OF HER MOTHER'S death, at sixty, from breast cancer, my grandmother says only that a doctor in the South of France recommended that her mother eat ham for its curative properties, causing indignation and anxiety, as no one knew whether the directive was inspired by antisemitism or scientific fact.

"Did she eat it?"

"No. It was much too late, anyway. The cancer had erupted through the skin. I think there was dropsy." Hypochondriac that she is, my grandmother plants gruesome— and, history will prove, indelible—images of death and disease in my head.

"What's dropsy?"

"It's—oh, I don't know. Your toes weep."

"What do you mean, they weep? How can they?"

"I mean they swell up until they are about to burst and the water comes through the skin."

Aside from the imagined pathogenesis of everything from snail fever to dropsy and hiccups that go on until they become lethal, my grandmother reports surreal and grotesque deaths. She explains her refusal to use an escalator as the inevitable result of the mishap of an unnamed, possibly apocryphal cousin who, having fallen on a set of moving stairs, was delivered to the bottom, where the stairs flatten and disappear, and in the case of the unfortunate cousin snatched up her slip and her blouse and her ribbons and hair and pulled them into the underworld while turning her over and over like a hot dog on greasy rollers until she was stripped naked and flayed to death. A girlhood friend stepped on a needle that entered her bloodstream and, accelerating in tandem with her panicked pulse, arrived at her heart, pierced it, and killed her.

All my grandmother says of her father's death is that he succumbed to grief, an opinion shared by many: ". . . his heart was elsewhere, and one can but hope that he has attained that content for which each of us strives," reads a condolence card from a relative in Australia, who said of my great-grandfather that he was "a good man, simple and benevolent," a man who had sustained all the loss he could.

"The dearest man," George tells me. "There wasn't a soul who didn't like him, nor a person in need he didn't help."

THE BOYS NEXT door poke a stick through the bottom of a mockingbird's nest, and three hatchlings tumble out and fall on the lawn below. It's not grass anymore but Dichondra, tiny flat green leaves that aren't blades but round and flat like Lilliputian lily pads. It doesn't need mowing—that's the whole point of it—so my grandfather tells Diego not to bring Santo back, but goes on giving him money surreptitiously.

Only one hatchling survives. The broken nest hangs from a branch of the olive tree outside the French doors between my mother's room and the garden, not far from one of our three birdbaths. My grandmother is a birder, but not a proper one. She doesn't go out looking for birds but uses binoculars to peer at the ones that visit her feeder, and she doesn't use her Audubon guide to check off the Southern California species she's seen. Instead she renames them. There is no chickadee for her, instead the Lilly Daché, because the markings on the bird's head recall the black "circle hat" introduced by Daché, milliner to the stars. My grandmother has two Daché hats. The robin's puffed red breast turns him into the Scarlet Pimpernel.

"What's a Scarlet Pimpernel?"

"Who."

"All right, who is the Scarlet Pimpernel?"

He is Sir Percy, the leader of a secret band of aristocrats who go to France during the Revolution and rescue other aristocrats before they can be guillotined. A baroness made them up. *The Scarlet Pimpernel* and *The Elusive Pimpernel* and *The Triumph* and *The Way of the Scarlet Pimpernel.*

"Isn't Sir Percy like Robin Hood, only for rich people?"

"No, because he isn't a thief."

"What is he, then?"

"A hero, of course."

Anything tufted is a Skeezix, referring to the comic-strip character's cowlick. The smallest of the sparrows are Cheese Mites. The hooded oriole is television's Dr. Kildare; no longer are there fickle little finches but Once-for-Love-and-Twice-for-Moneys, in homage to a friend's matrimonial history. Townsend's warblers are Ritzas, in honor of Wee-Wee-de-la-Ritza, the name my grandmother gave to a lapdog belonging to an opera singer she met at the Plaza Athénée in 1930. The dog made a habit of urinating on the hotel's drapes. The entire name is code for "Something smells bad."

"No one said a word. The concierge went on smiling. Floor-length silk moiré drapes. That's how famous she was, and how much money she had."

"What was her name?"

"Something de la Ritza. I can't remember."

"What kind of dog was Wee-Wee?"

"Small."

It's not only renaming the animals; my grandmother must take possession of the language, alter its parts to make it hers alone. A flea is a *fleak,* a pimple a *punckle,* old people—she doesn't consider herself among them—are *winks.* If the letter *L* is at the beginning of a word, it is replaced by *Y. Yet's go to the Yickle Yibrary. Ickle* is peculiar to *yickle*. Spittle isn't *spickle*; brittle is not *brickle*. But belittle is *beyickle*, despite the *L* following a prefix beginning with *B*. Like all languages, my grandmother's has rules, exceptions, and surprises. Here and there a bit of cockney creeps in: *Oh the dear yickle fing!* is her customary response to almost anything with fur.

I use a tissue as a sling to move the hatchling into a nest I made of shredded tissues and a shoebox. It has so little down it might as well be naked. Its head is all black eyeballs looking through their lids and a beak that isn't a beak yet, with the wet red corners of lips. I can see its insistent little heart, not red at all, nor the shape of a valentine, but a tiny black fist punching under what's thinner than onionskin. There is no suggestion that such a creature will ever fly, and I am not so young that I don't know how fast shoebox turns into casket.

Birds dive at our sliding glass doors—mourning doves mostly; the occasional Cad-and-a-Bounder, the jays that chase down poor old Mitzi to seize bits of her fur as nest lining. I make tinfoil raptors and hang them on strings in front of each door to startle the birds away from the mirage, but they don't help, not as they do with the fruit trees. There's no way to prevent the glass from reflecting the garden. My grandfather tells me most of the birds break their necks and die right away, and that dying doesn't hurt. Sometimes a little blood leaks out from between the feathers on their breasts, and the beauty of its color seizes my heart. All of them must have proper burials.

"Did you touch it?" my mother says when she sees the hatchling.

"I tried not to." The dead babies are where they fell but under the ground now, under a mound of dirt decorated by a ring of pebbles. I didn't have another box, so there are only the two tissue shrouds in the one shared grave.

"You must have touched the Kleenex." She looks at me, and I ready myself for whatever comes next. But she isn't angry; she's looking past me at the olive branch on the other side of the glass. Olives make you sick unless soaked in salt-water for however long it takes to draw the poison out. My grandfather told me this, lest I should take it into my head to eat one off the tree.

"The mother wouldn't have come back anyway," my mother says. "The nest is too broken to fix."

After she tries and fails to get the baby bird to eat egg yolk, either raw or cooked—she puts a dab on the torn end of a paper match—she calls the zoo. The ornithologist tells my mother that the red corners of the hatchling's mouth are those of a soft-billed bird who will never eat seeds, and before I can ask my grandfather to dig up a worm to feed him, the ornithologist says don't bother, a bird so young can't survive. No matter what we do, he promises her it can't, not without its own mother.

"He *promised?*" I don't like the word used on looming catastrophes.

"Yes."

But the hatchling does live. My mother takes him (whom we call a *he* by default; we don't know if he's a boy) to work in the shoebox and hides it on a heating pad under her desk, and this does not make the lawyers for whom she works angry, as I expect them to be. I don't see what she is, not to them. I don't see a beautiful girl who types fifty words a minute without mistakes and seventy-five if she goes as fast as she possibly can. I don't see her immaculate desk, the continuously emptied in-box, the yellow pad covered with shorthand as regular as a machine's. All I know is that the bird between her feet cannot be hidden, as its voice gives it away.

I HAVE ORDERED them by year—1908, 1909, 1910, 1912—to rehearse what I know: my grandmother was nine years old in 1908, ten in 1909, eleven in 1910 . . . Every Christmas for a decade the sisters each received one volume of Andrew Lang's Fairy Books, always a new color—*Red, Grey, Violet, Blue, Brown, Green*—so many that Mr. Lang didn't take the trouble, it seems to me, to think up titles. A random sampling suggests it is true, what I suspect: hundreds of fairy tales written by the same person amount to redundancy; magic runs out, as there are only so many new things a fairy can do. All the volumes are inscribed, either "With Love to Darling Peggy from Her Mother" or "With Love to Darling Cecily from Her Mother." The fairy tales traveled from a bookseller in London to Shanghai, where they were inscribed by my great-grandmother and then mailed back to London in time to put under Uncle Arthur's tree. The Isaacs, into whose family my grandmother's mother's sister, Anne, had married, also were Jews who turned their backs on Hanukkah. "Christmas is more fun for the children," my grandmother says about what I can tell has nothing to do with the excitement of opening more than one gift at a time.

"Why do you have some of Aunt Cecily's books?"

"She gave me some of hers, after."

"When you got out of the fever hospital?"

"Yes."

As consumed as she is by fears of ailments she hasn't yet had, she dismisses the ones she has had, as if they are too pedestrian to warrant her attention. In 1908 an epidemic of scarlet fever emptied London boarding schools and filled hospital beds, among them one in the London Fever Hospital, where my grandmother lay for the better part of a month, head shaved.

"And then you found out they'd taken all your books and your toys and burned them all up with your clothes."

My grandmother perches on the side of the tub, washcloth at the ready. "Your skin comes off after the fever's over and the rash fades," she says. "The skin comes off your hands all in one piece—"

"Like a snake."

"Like a glove, I was going to say."

Ill enough to be in a hospital, quarantined and bereft of visitors, stripped of every book and toy, with only stubble left of her long dark hair, thousands of miles from her mother and father: She speaks of a thing so terrible as if it were nothing. Just as my grandfather reports how, when he was fourteen and alone in Berlin, "a big fat *schutzmann*"—a policeman—"with a big sword, helmeted, with a spike," lay in wait for him every day, taunted him as he went back and forth to his lodgings. Called my grandfather names he will not repeat to me, that's how bad they were.

"Weren't you frightened?" I ask my grandmother.

"Well, I didn't think I was going to die, if that's what you mean."

"But your heart started to murmur, and never stopped."

She shrugs, uninterested.

"I DON'T THINK you really want me to."

"I do!"

"Last time you were sorry."

"But I'm different now. I know I am!"

"How?"

"Last time I was eight, not nine!"

I ask, I wheedle, I beg, he concedes. He knows I am not different but everlastingly the same, and so do I, and yet he conspires with me. We are together in this mistake. From the side of the swimming pool I watch him, chin level with the water's surface, legs dangling below. Wavelets on the surface make them wobble like a jellyfish's tentacles.

"Now!" I say as the second hand of his wristwatch touches on XII, and he blows all the air from his lungs and allows himself to sink to the bottom of the deep end, where he sits over the drain, legs crossed like my own. *Bulova,* says the face hanging from my wrist, the second hand a gold needle that spurs my heart even as it holds him under the surface of the water. I don't know why I ask him to do this terrible thing, only that I can't help it. By the time he pushes off from the bottom—the water flat as glass, his legs straight like a man's—returns to the surface, and gasps, I am crying.

I never see the white hair on his chest, or how that chest

is bony where other fathers have muscles. I don't see wrinkles or liver spots or fingers gnarled by arthritis. What I do is, I add up his two legs to make a second heart, should the first one fail.

"SIX MONTHS! AND I didn't miss a single day, not one."

To hear my grandmother tell it, the five years she lived in London—from 1934, when her father died and she moved out of Villa Edgerton, until 1939, when she left Old World for New—are adequately represented by the first six months, when she visited Tony, her Boston bulldog, every day while he was quarantined, as then legally required for the prevention of rabies. Tony was quite old by then, acquired before her mother fell ill. He belonged to a period of freedom, when she had yet to mourn any loss so keen, and was the first of my grandmother's pets to receive her fanatical attention.

Tony, Villa Edgerton, 1932.

No longer tethered to ailing parents, the sisters closed the villa, drawing its heavy velvet curtains against the Mediterranean light. They split the Chinese antiquities, divided the Persian rugs, and each took what furniture she wanted; the remainder was auctioned off. With trust funds of equal value, they went their separate ways.

My grandmother, thirty-five, moved herself across the Channel and took over the apartment the family kept in London, at 19 St. James's Square before moving to a flat on Cheyne Walk. Overlooking the Thames, Cheyne Walk was a string of exclusive addresses, home at various times to Dante Gabriel Rossetti, Bertrand Russell, and John Barrymore. It is where George Eliot died, at 4 Cheyne Walk. Of these years my grandmother says little, other than to repeat what has become a family saying, unwittingly coined by her uncle Arthur, her mother's brother-in-law, in whose home she was born and with whom the sisters spent their winter holidays.

As my great-grandfather had asked him to do after his death, Arthur Isaacs managed what my grandmother calls her affairs, referring to those of a financial type, but his guidance ruled her romantic life as well. Almost sixty, he had the gravitas to dispatch "poor prospects"—for London had its share of destitute aristocrats looking for a rich woman who wanted to be addressed as Duchess or Marchioness. In this capacity, Arthur famously rebuffed one gold digger with a line that has become family code for any undesirable attachment: "You've got no looks! You've got no money! Tell me, what have you got!"

This doesn't have to refer to a person—you can just as well say it to a dog or a chair or a pudding—but you have to say it as you imagine he would, with a sort of rotund and oratorical English accent.

IF SOLOMON SASSOON Benjamin failed to select the man my grandmother would marry, he did end in choosing where she'd live for all her married life. My grandmother moved to Los Angeles because it was the only American city she could picture herself in—the only one she had ever visited apart from her brief stay in San Francisco, when the Sassoons and the Kadoories were making their slow, adventurous way back to China.

Six weeks after the armistice, my grandmother's father took her on the kind of trip that happens in nineteenth-century novels, in which girls with broken engagements are sent off to Baden-Baden or another climate considered curative, with healthful distractions. They stayed in Pasadena, which she remembers as "nothing but orange groves, every way you looked acre upon acre of oranges," an exotic fruit to a girl who lived in Shanghai when she wasn't in London. California land was yet unspoiled, even primeval: truly a fresh new world, where her father wangled an invitation for her to ride in the Rose Parade, on a horse decked out in Mexican silver.

For my grandmother there was only Los Angeles; the rest of the United States was uncharted territory. Or, put another way, no land existed but that within her father's purview.

ON SEPTEMBER 3, 1939, Britain declared war on Germany and women and children began to be evacuated from London. Within two weeks my grandmother had a United States green card, which identified her as one of the 132,000 Jews allowed to immigrate during the entire Second World War. One hundred and thirty-two thousand was only 10 percent of the United States' legal quota on immigrants, and my grandmother alludes to the strings her uncle Arthur pulled, strings so secret he couldn't tell her about the collecting of papers and signatures, stamps.

All of it has left her with an indelible fear of leaving the United States and not being allowed back in for some reason, she doesn't know what: that's the way it works. Because if you did know what, you could get back in. Equally terrorizing is the idea of something happening to her *papers*—she pronounces the word with a tone of dread and awe, and pays to keep them at the bank in a fireproof box—a loss that will result in the revocation of her citizenship. My grandmother may have come of age in a lawless treaty port that cared nothing for passports or any form of identification, but outside of Shanghai she was fixed on the potential of lost documents to spell tragedy and death.

Cecily, trapped in occupied Paris, had nothing between her and the SS but false papers procured by Mlle. Garrigues, a Catholic—as was Cecily herself since 1930, which convinced my grandmother that Catholicism is a side effect of lesbianism. Or a code: an announcement of sapphic tendencies.

I know better than to pursue an *idée fixe*. She's got it wrong, though. Catholicism is a side effect of Judaism, another expression of whatever it is that turns a *Halem* into a *Bottomly*.

The story of the false papers, procured in the nick of time, is filled with slavering Alsatians (my grandmother never calls them German shepherds), bribed officials, a purloined letter from a personage in Lyon, and a sexual assault accepted by Mlle. Garrigues for what it was: another form of payment.

IMMEDIATELY UPON HER arrival in Los Angeles, my grandmother's Wafer diaries, made by Smythson's of London, are too small to accommodate her new life, allowing a day but two square inches, fifteen or twenty words scribbled in faded pencil. Even my sharp eyes, useful for threading needles, struggle here. The entries are not for me to read; I find them by stealth on a solitary afternoon, my grandmother out, my grandfather gardening. I find them in my grandmother's cedar chest, which I know better than to open. Although it has a lock, she doesn't lock it, so the trespass seems less criminal. I have entered but not broken. The rubber bands that bind each decade of diaries tightly together are so old they crumble at my touch. The years are hidden away in chronological order. The pressure of reducing a day to a single line—whether that day was "breathtaking!" or "rain, rain, and nothing else"—summons a spare eloquence that is at odds with my grandmother, the embroiderer. She lunches out, she dines out, she sees—and succinctly reviews—three movies a week: *"Grapes of Wrath*: rotten story. *Victor Herbert* great. *The Shop Around the Corner* V good!"* She had cousins in San Francisco and a handful of old friends in Los Angeles who had emigrated from Europe before she did. She knew enough people and was gregarious enough to soon know many more and reports a quiet day as "nothing much" or "stayed in." But there were not many quiet days, never more than one a week, unless she was ill with a cold, when she took to bed with a level of concern others save for pneumonia.

Lunch at the Brown Derby, dinner at Chasen's, lunch at the Swiss Chalet and dinner in, with an extra pair of hands to wait table. A visit to an Arab horse ranch, the fantasy of buying a horse tethering her to 1919.

She comments on the weather daily, as she would aloud. In my grandmother's binary reports, either a day is fine or it is dull. It is wet or dry. It is hot or cold. She hates wind, stays in, draws the curtains. Curiously, her terse reports mirror those of the 5th Battalion's war diaries during my grand-father's time in Annappes: Cloudy. Dull and showery. Fine. Wet. Dry. Wind. Underlined with displeasure; I can tell by how fast the pencil moved, her angry slash.

Restless, my grandmother is fixed on the possibilities of each day and how weather might impede or enhance them. It's the same as with parasites and contagion. Though she has turned her back on China, left it many years and miles ago, she is followed by a typhoon. All the way to the Riviera, where it snatched away her mother and father, and then across another ocean and another continent, its mani-fest destiny to chase her to sunny California, where a storm summons her to the window and draws her dark eyebrows together.

"Why do you?"

"Why do I what?"

"Hate wind?"

She's silent and then, after a moment, tells me it's mostly a March wind she dislikes, her mother having died on March 7, her father on March 14.

"Why would it bother you if you were inside?"

"Oh, you know. Bent-over trees, leaves rushing past the windowpanes. That sound under the eaves."

After that I'm not afraid of wind but fixed on it as something that might separate a soul from its body. If I see it's started to blow, I run to stand under the avocado tree, so I can look up and watch the leaves move as they speak in rushed secrets. Sibilant, but not like a snake's slithery, earthbound tongue; this is different, a buoyant language, out of reach. Alive and rushing all about me, lifting the hair from my head and raising gooseflesh on my arms. If I close my eyes I can almost understand it, Christian Science: A wind, not any old wind but a holy wind, will blow right through me, it will sieve out my soul and leave the dross of my body. I'll be aloft.

IT'S FALL WHEN we release him, six months old and unhappy as a captive. We let him out of his cage to fly around the house, but it isn't enough for him; he bumps his head on the ceiling. Outside, as it is Los Angeles, trees are lush, their leaves green year-round. He disappears quickly among them. For a week he remains within sight of our house. He doesn't come when called, and as he mimics other birds there's no point in listening for him, but soon my eye is trained to see the flash of white when he opens his wings, and for a week or so I can sometimes find him among the leaves. And then one day I can't, and it is followed by another.

First I am inconsolable. Next I refuse to be consoled. It's an echo of my mother's departure, after which I punish myself both for losing her and for being grateful for the peace of her absence. The part of me that remains faithful to the conceit of my child-mother's sudden embrace of motherhood anticipates her brief visits with excited dread. Because however it goes, it goes wrong. Of necessity it goes wrong. Whoever accompanies her, boyfriend or girl, I hate categorically. If it's a boyfriend, whoever he is, he regards me with palpable righteous objection: I am an unfortunate complication, my existence an impediment to wooing. It's not that she's kept me a secret but that I am suddenly corporeal, no longer an idea but a fact: my mother has a daughter in the care of her aged parents. Whoever he is, should he choose my mother, he is likely to inherit me. Romance often cools at this juncture, but what can she do, keep me a secret? All the pretty dresses in the world cannot save my mother from the fact of me. If I've made the mistake of running toward her car, I stop when she gets out and the glare of her dismay shows me my tangled hair, missing barrette, dirty, ragged fingernails and dirty clothes, dirt and grass stains everywhere. The few boyfriends who pretend friendly interest in me do so only in front of my mother. The one who seems to regard me as an asset has oily hands. I can't bring myself to look at his face.

If it's a girlfriend my mother has the sense, born of experience, to protect her from my grandmother, who, though never profane, has proven her ability to terrorize even the forewarned. With respect to verbal sparring, were there an equivalent to the Marquess of Queensberry's Rules, my grandmother would be barred from participation. It's not only that she consistently hits below the belt. Watching her take down prey is little different from seeing a lioness leaping to open an antelope's jugular on Mutual of Omaha's *Wild Kingdom*: cruel and efficient, in the way of animals. Her means don't so much justify her ends as they dramatically and shamelessly deliver her to victory. To secure an advantage she has locked herself in her room and howled a victim into submission, confident that, in the case of Ingrid, the girl would run away and never come back. Even my mother was shocked into silence. It isn't that she wouldn't expect such a thing from my grandmother—anyone who knows her well would—but the animal aggression of it, and the talent my grandmother has for screaming, and most of all her readiness to terrorize by means of so antisocial a talent: no one forgets one of my grandmother's screams, its power increased by her invisibility. They suggest a larger person suffering the kind of madness that burns houses down, like Mr. Rochester's wife did Thornfield Hall.

SHE'D LIVED IN Los Angeles for six months. She owned a house at 360 Hilgard Avenue and had furnished it with heirlooms—the sideboard, the clocks, the dining room table and chairs, her mother's chaise longue, her father's armchair (my grandfather's now), the fire dogs, the Ming vases, the sterling platters, carved ivories, and eight Persian rugs, all shipped from London. She "interviewed skivvies" for days; she hired one who was "nothing to write home about." She got about with a hired car and driver until she had her own car—a touring car, a Packard convertible.

My grandmother to the left of her cousin Marjorie, Yosemite, 1940.

Then, as soon as she had unpacked her trunks of clothes and set everything neatly in her dresser drawers, freshly lined with scented paper, she pulled out a suitcase, filled it, and set off to do what she loved most.

On March 27, 1940, she was "Packed! V V excited!" for her first tour of the California "countryside." The next day she left at dawn for San Bernardino, where she breakfasted, and then continued east to Las Vegas. There she spent two nights and took a day trip to Boulder Dam (renamed the Hoover Dam in 1947). "Simply wonderful sight! Then looked around. Went back to Las Vegas."

It wasn't Monaco, it didn't have the sea, but there was something that drew her to it, a place fueled by money and made for the shameless meeting of voyeurs and exhibitionists. But it was frantic, frenetic, and stayed up all night; she'd had enough of it after two days and set out into the desert, the convertible's top down, for the Inn at Furnace

Creek. A hundred and fifty miles of desert: "Beautiful! But bad and dangerous roads." It was spring, and the same rains that washed out highways had let loose cataracts of wild-flowers; streams of purple and yellow tumbled through dry boulders.

"Arrived 2 p.m. Looked around. Rested." The inn had a warm spring-fed swimming pool, catered to more than a sprinkling of movie stars and a gangster or two. She could lie on a chaise by the pool for only so long, though. The next day she was back in the car, crisscrossing the rain shadow of the Mojave, getting out to look at the twisted arms of the Joshua trees, the white yucca flowers that towered over her head. "Gorgeous!" Then she was at the top of the Panamint range, looking out over Death Valley.

Seven hundred and fifty miles of stopping at every scenic point, spending a night where fancy took her, spending another, or not, driving on: she was, as she wrote wherever she went, "looking around." Not looking for. Even so, she'd found something. She'd transplanted her life from Europe—touring the Alps, stopping at Lake Como, taking a jaunt to the Jungfrau—to a new continent, a state that fulfilled its golden promise.

Complete with a recherché spa.

MY GRANDFATHER'S BECOMING an American wasn't a dramatic experience, as it was for my grandmother. It didn't feel like a change so much as a confirmation of what was already true: he'd lived in the United States' territories, worked toward Alaska's development, surveyed land for its railroad, helped engineer its bridges. If he wasn't a citizen of the United States, he was an Alaskan.

"People are rough up there, but so generous—they'd give you everything, a lot of them, they never lock their doors." He calls Alaska a "marvelous human equation," and when I ask what he means, he says that if you're on the trail, far away from anywhere else, you have to leave your cabin door open. "You are obliged to leave it open with enough wood and supplies."

"And matches?"

"Matches kept dry in a jar. Canned food. A pail for collecting snow to melt into water."

He'd made his way, mile by mile, toward the thing he was looking for, whatever it was; he'd know when he found it. When he ran out of west, he flipped a coin and followed it north, and there it was, at last, beauty that did him violence, tore at his heart, a land as brutal as it was beautiful, presenting dangers that wrung generosity from even the mean-spirited.

I can tell by the timbre of his voice, the way it tilts north when he speaks of it, north like a compass needle, north toward crystalline years cleaved into dark and light. North, as far north as possible, to where your lungs freeze if you run ten steps. It's like Moses's burning bush or the frozen pole you must not touch lest it flay you: you are too close to God.

My grandfather never returned to Alaska after the war. The years he lived in Alaska represent but a tenth of his life, but they crowd the rest out of his mind. For him, the territory remained pristine, land so powerful he'd never imagine its being tamed and drilled for oil, bleeding into a different human equation that would force it to hasten its own death, greed my grandfather unwittingly served, working on the railway, pushing it toward statehood and depredation.

For a man who kept flawless ledgers, his jump on figures was of no help to his own finances. He had a guilelessness obvious to grifters. In Prince George a man offered him a chance to make some money by investing in supplies to peddle downriver.

"At different camps," my grandfather says. "Fifteen, twenty, a hundred miles down the river. Like a fool, I gave him the six hundred dollars I'd saved, and that was the last I ever saw of it!" He laughs about this, as he does about other such mishaps. (But not about his being cheated out of a pension when he retired from McGregor-Doniger Sportswear. I'm not supposed to know about it, but there's a sheaf of correspondence between my grandfather and "Old Man Doniger," creamy thick sheets embossed with a tiny swatch of red-and-green tartan.)

Growing up poor doesn't inspire avarice in my grandfather, nor does it make him a miser. Instead it seems to have left him uninterested in money.

Or perhaps it's the doing of Alaska.

Money has little value in the land where he is happiest. Everything is different where the sun never sets. Strawberries get to be "as big as baseballs" before they ripen and turn red. Flowers grow around the clock until they are as tall as houses; they grow so fast they have no time for perfume, only color. And the cities are made of tents and the houses are in the wilderness, and no one owns them, not as they do here.

HAVING RELOCATED MY grandmother, tended to her "affairs," and overseen the purchase of her new home in Los Angeles, Arthur Isaacs remained in California for another ten months, until, on July 5, 1940, "Darling of darlings suddenly left us down at Coronado, left us stunned and stricken."

They were having brunch at a favorite restaurant, the Hotel del Coronado, just across the bay from San Diego, when Arthur's heart stopped between the first and second bites of his eggs Benedict. I want to know if he fell over onto the table or stayed sitting up in his seat, but I can't ask, as a diary I am not supposed to be reading prompts the question.

Arthur Isaacs, 1930.

For months, on into August and September, my grandmother is submerged in grief. She has lost "the best friend and protector I ever had." Her diary mentions no films, no lunches out, no shopping, no exploring her new home. Instead she drives the twenty miles to and from the Home of Peace Cemetery, the oldest Jewish cemetery in Los

Angeles, and goes to temple every Friday evening. "Sad," she writes. "Long dreary sad day." "Tired and worn out from sadness."

She went to temple for all three now: her mother, father, and uncle. She went alone and recited the Kaddish. For her, faith is mourning. Or it was. By the time I am born, my grandmother has given up going to services of any kind and is firmly dug into her opinion that religion causes more trouble than it's worth. She has her own rituals.

Every summer we have brunch at the Hotel Del. Uncle Arthur calls us back to the great room of sparkling windows looking over the sea. Sunday brunch was his favorite meal of the week, eggs Benedict his favorite dish, which my grandparents always order. Grateful to be excused from eggs, I cut my French toast with care, keep my left hand in my lap, and am seen and not heard. Technically I am not supposed to be in fancy restaurants, but as my grandmother makes the rules, she can overlook them.

ON SUNDAY, APRIL 20, 1941, my grandmother "went down to Harry Jacobs' for supper. Pleasant evening."

It must have been a first date, as it is the single time she uses my grandfather's surname. From that point forward he is Harry, often followed by G.B.H.S.—*God Bless His Soul.* They met when seated together at a dinner party by a hopeful matchmaker, one so reductive in her methods that a shared British accent was reason enough to expect shared sensibilities. My grandmother would have noted what her hostess and the other people around the table didn't hear—my grandfather had a not-quite-Cockney accent. Americans (for once making a useful blunder) couldn't tell the difference between her plummy aristocratic tone and his, which wasn't so East End that he pronounced *bother* "bover" or said "dis fing" for *this thing.*

All the others gathered around the table saw a handsome widower, whose elegant clothes—his trade demanded he be au courant—didn't hide his callused hands, permanently hewn by hard labor. Dark blond going white, blue eyes. At fifty he was nine years my grandmother's elder, and at five-eleven nine inches taller, his skin fair where hers would be brown if she sunbathed.

"Talked," her Wafer diary reports.

"Spent the whole time talking."

"Went for a drive and talked."

"Met at Farmers Market for lunch. Talked."

"Picnicked at Torrey Pines. Talked."

She would have been discreet about her past, and he about his. I know that much without eavesdropping on little diaries. It was easy to avoid speaking of past attachments

My grandfather and grandmother at Torrey Pines, La Jolla, 1941.

when they both had exotic backgrounds. She told him stories about Shanghai. He told her about Alaska.

My grandfather would not have recognized the name Sassoon; still, my grandmother always presented herself as the foreign aristocrat she was. Not that she said so, at least not in words. She had the posture and carriage of her caste, her accent that of the British marchioness she never became;

her French was flawless. And, as people said about her father, she was "jolly good fun"—witty, with a lively repertoire of risqué limericks, a woman whose carnal gaze could not be frozen by film. Photographs of her communicate a desire decades old, if not dead. A snob, but not in the expected ways, she'd leave a party to "talk with the skivvies" if the skivvies were more interesting than the partygoers.

For my grandfather, the exotic princess was redeemed by her industry, the restless energy that drove her to the Red Cross every Monday, where she knit socks for as long as eight hours, recording the experience in her diary with as much enthusiasm as she would a holiday diversion. Week after week of Mondays: "Red Cross all day!" and "enjoyed it immensely!"

She could easily overlook my grandfather's accent, especially as she had discovered something of far more consequence in the quiet widower spellbound by her past: he had long ago relinquished his attachment to the sort of Jews who give Jews a bad name.

"What does that mean, Jews who give Jews a bad name?"

I know she's not going to answer the question, not directly. It's more likely to inspire a bitter memory of, for example, the parking valet who called her Cadillac convertible a "Jew canoe" on the heels of another who called it a Cad*jew*llac, inspiring—forcing—her to trade the car she loved for one she loves less. None of these stories explain my grandmother's prejudice so much as they represent a binary hierarchy. Among Jews, there are but two kinds: her kind—Mizrahi—and the rest, who give hers a bad name, the ones buried downhill in the Hong Kong cemetery, the ones who were by 1941 vilified by Nazi caricatures of hook-nosed, beady-eyed degenerates who drank the blood of Christian babies, who smashed her baby brother's headstone, and from one continent to another dragged *kikes, shysters,* and *shylocks* behind them. These reviled Jews don't summon more sympathy from my grandmother than any other persecuted group. She feels, perhaps, no more kinship with them than she would with a "black African." Not only are they not of her blood or heritage, they are a personal affront: how can it be that people do not recognize what separates her from the vulgar throng clamoring for lox at Nate 'n Al's? Better to be called a wog in England than a hymie in the United States.

My grandfather, soft-spoken, unassuming, the last man to "Jew a man down," had given up his problematic birthright for his wife's Christian Science, one of the handful of fin-de-siècle New Thought movements that eased assimilation while leaving Jesus at a comfortable remove. All of it boiled down to mind over matter, or the apotheosis of denial—the only evil being the evil we perceive as we fall into error.

My grandmother is, when she wants to be, a good sport. Her diaries record that she accompanied my grandfather to "Xian Science church" for a year, as she relaxed her attention to mourning in a synagogue. It didn't last, not after she was pregnant.

I never ask the question, either aloud or to myself in silence, how, after watching his wife die in agony and without help, my grandfather didn't turn his back on a faith that not only blamed the woman he loved for dying but punished her for it, denying her relief from pain.

I don't know how, but I do know why. All through his long life, mind-over-matter positivism served my grandfather as nothing else had—carried him out of misfortune and into what he always called "opportunity," buoyed him across an ocean and over wastelands of ice, tested him and called him north toward all that answered his longing. Beauty that was frozen, incorruptible.

IL N'Y A PAS *d'amour, il n'y a que des preuves d'amour.* "There is no love, there are only the proofs thereof." It's among my grandmother's favorite aphorisms, and she does tally the ephemera of love.

She records each telephone call when my grandfather is away, on the road, as she does the receipt of his letters. The latter is in part the habit of a woman used to waiting for packet ships from Europe, counting the days since she had sent a letter to calculate how many more it might be until she received a reply. But it's more than that, for my grandfather is not on the other side of the world, and it is not necessary to record each phone call or whether there was one or two that day.

On May 10, 1941, my grandmother writes, "Had nice evening with Harry. Drove to Venice, and Santa Monica, where the great question was asked, and accepted." They had known each other for forty days, in contact if not together on every one of them. The next day, May 11, a Sunday, she had "a lovely day on the beach with Harry and then we came back and had supper. How happy I am." Monday morning she was off "with singing in my heart to the Red Cross. Harry came up after dinner and we went for a short drive." Tuesday, "Harry was away in San Bernardino, did nothing special, missed him." Wednesday, "Harry phoned me. Went down to his house in the evening and we ate and talked. I am so so happy."

When they met downtown for lunch, "it was grand." "Harry came for dinner, bless him." "Lunch at the Farmers Market together." "H came in after dinner—so glad to see him!" "Spent a gorgeous day together—picnic in Del Mar." "Fetched H to dinner, GBHS." "Another gorgeous day, H spent the whole day with me. I am so happy and in love."

It must be a powerful thing, a thing hard for me to imagine, that can transform my tart grandmother into a person who goes about tallying up telephone calls with singing in her heart. The wedding is set for September 3, 1941, in Las Vegas, which seems a place reserved for impulsive unions, soon regretted and dissolved, but, dependable in her ability to simultaneously flout and serve convention, my grandmother elopes with a trousseau. For months her Wafer diary reports weekly pilgrimages to Saks and I. Magnin for peignoirs and other lingerie, and each Wednesday an appointment with a dressmaker. For the exchange of vows—"The great day! Harry and I were spliced at noon by Justice Brown! Lovely ceremony!"—she wears a burgundy suit with padded shoulders and a veiled burgundy hat, gloves, and pumps. It seems odd to elope at such an age. Even I know it's for teenagers, like Romeo and Juliet, whose parents won't let them get married. She was forty-two and he fifty-one. It does until I remember the Lanvin gown with the six-foot train, all the letters of apology to accompany returned presents.

"Ridiculous," she says when I ask. "At our age! Me dressing up in white and asking for flatware!"

The choice of Las Vegas must have been my grandmother's, for she was firmly established in her route, now two years old, on which Las Vegas was a stop.

"Too vulgar to catch on" is a phrase that slips into conversation among the grown-ups, shorthand for a mistake of incalculable proportion. Some years after they marry, my grandfather was offered the chance to buy a block of the Las Vegas strip. They'd have to sacrifice Sunset, fire the architect, sell 11027 when it was yet a toeless hill waiting to be topped. Las Vegas was "too vulgar to catch on," he told my grandmother. It made more sense to invest the money in a house.

The day after the wedding they were in Lone Pine, then Reno, Lake Tahoe, Grass Valley, Sacramento, Santa Maria, San Francisco, each place greeted with the same childlike excitement. "Gorgeous drive!" "Went over the Donner Pass to Nevada City and had a grand time!"

In Sacramento my grandmother dropped my grandfather and his sample cases off for a sales call and tooled around in the car by herself. It wasn't a Hispano-Suiza but a Pontiac convertible, and she was not in the Jungfrau contemplating St. Moritz but driving through California's Sierra Nevada— for her, more exotic than the familiar Alps.

"So ends the one and only trip of a person's life," my grandmother writes in the little diary's space for memoranda.

The route of a traveling salesman enchanting a Sassoon princess: it's not that she isn't a snob, because she assuredly is, but her snobbery is like all the rest of her: it suits her fancy. If a traveling salesman accidentally managed the trick of replicating what she'd most loved about Europe—touring in an automobile—then a traveling salesman was the obvious choice for someone so restless that she was happiest in a car, neither here nor there but on her way.

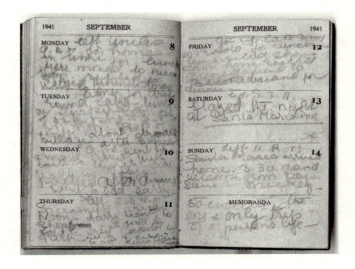

AS ACCIDENTS GO, it's not dramatic. My grandfather is driving me to school when the brakes fail. He turns out of traffic; we go down an embankment and hit one of the towering eucalyptus that border the UCLA campus; the hood crumples like a paper fan.

It doesn't hurt, not at all, and we get out of the car. My grandfather's face doesn't say anything when he presses his handkerchief to my mouth. It turns red quickly and, saturated, drips blood onto the pavement, spattering the toes of my white saddle oxfords. Still, I am not afraid until I push it away to talk and all that comes out of my mouth is blood. I look up at him, feel it sliding warm and thick down the back of my throat, and see his expression change as he bends down to pick me up.

Then there's the sound of tires on gravel and the sound of a car door slamming, one I recognize as well as I do her tread on the stairs. No one slams a car door quite like my mother. It's not what I let myself believe, that the power of my spilled blood has summoned my mother, nor is it a freakish coincidence, as every morning she takes Sunset Boulevard to get to work at the same time that my grandfather uses it to take me to school, just in different directions. We saw her at a stoplight once, and my grandfather honked and I waved, but she was putting on eye makeup in the rearview mirror.

.   .   .

They decide my grandfather will wait for a tow truck and my mother will take me to the emergency room at UCLA, minutes away—a disastrous division of labor as far as I'm concerned. My mother hands me over to a nurse and says she is going away, she has to call her boss and tell him why she's late. All I understand is that she's leaving, and I am so afraid that I forget my own address. *Eleven oh two seven* is gone. Only *Sunset* is left in my head.

By the time she returns I've been sedated. They had to, the nurse tells her, and she reports my slide into a panic that bit the doctor. It's not enough that I have disgraced myself as a Christian Scientist; when tested by forces other than myself I am not even human. A little animal, my mother calls me when I wake up at home. The same animal that pummeled the boy next door, I think. She tilts my chin one way and another.

"I don't think there will be much of a scar," she says, as though examining a broken saucer yet to be glued.

MY GRANDFATHER ASSUMED he and my grandmother would have a companionable, late-life marriage uncomplicated by children. He assumed my grandmother used birth control, and she gave him no reason to suspect she had no intention of using her diaphragm, which in any case she'd used a carpet needle to poke full of holes should an occasion demand its use. At forty-two, my grandmother intended to have a baby before it was too late and got pregnant so quickly—three months after my grandparents married—that it must have seemed as aberrant to my grandfather as it did to her obstetrician.

"I get all the freaks," he said of her being nearly forty-three when my mother was born, decades before medicine offered means of extending fertility into a woman's forties. My grandmother still repeats the words. *I get all the freaks.* They arise in conversation, or she says them aloud to herself and shakes her head. It's been nearly thirty years; she remains insulted. It was a delivery by cesarean section, followed by an emergency hysterectomy: fibroid tumors had grown along with my mother, com-

My grandmother and my mother, 1944.

peting for space in the womb. On September 8, 1942, when the obstetrician lifted my mother out, my grandmother began to hemorrhage, and thus lost the ability to have the second child she wanted. She remained in the hospital on bed rest for two weeks and returned home to the care of the nurse she'd engaged six weeks earlier, on August 3. There she continued on bed rest, only gradually returning to the life of an upright invalid. On October 12 the medical supply company retrieved the rented hospital bed and my grandmother returned to her usual life. She was in the car two days later, back at the movies the next night. Still, on October 24, the day after her forty-third birthday, she confessed that she was "still a bit tired" and went on saying so until it was determined that she suffered from an anemia particular to eastern Mediterranean peoples, a characteristic she passed on to me, along with her unmistakably Arab feet, leapfrogging over my mother, whose skin is perfectly milk-white, whereas mine is the sallow predicted by being one-sixteenth anemic Arab on my mother's side and one-sixteenth Apache on my father's.

So my grandfather was surprised by fatherhood twice, at fifty-two, when my mother was born, and at seventy-one when I arrived.

Not unhappy surprises, he makes sure I understand after I ask him what a classmate means by calling me an accident.

MARRIAGE, PARENTHOOD: MY grandparents don't settle down. They can't, neither of them.

She'd been up the Jungfrau and had now driven her car through a 2,300-year-old sequoia in Yosemite National Park (with a cousin). Over and over my grandmother's diaries record excitement at the prospect of setting out on what was becoming my grandparents' favorite route through the Sierra Nevada.

Years of correspondence home to my mother, left in the care of Libby, bear witness to my grandparents' setting out into the desert routinely, taking different routes to Death Valley, where my grandfather collected rocks he'd use to build the fishpond. They wrote and called home each day, they talked to my mother, but they didn't want her along.

My grandmother in particular did not want her child, the baby she had willed herself to have, to travel with her and her husband. Scores of photographs bear witness to my grandmother's delight in having a daughter, and she wrote to my mother every day she was away, long letters that include inventive stories about a family of mice. She spent hours loving my mother from afar, because children spoil vacations, snuff romance, ruin one's décolleté should one be so foolish as to nurse, and belong at home with their governesses.

Her idea of child-rearing was not only outdated, it depended on being able to afford a live-in, full-time governess, with a housekeeper to look after both the governess and her charge's needs. Later I'll wonder if this explains my mother's behavior—if it's the result of a well-intentioned mistake. She's not irresponsible; it's worse than that. There is a vengeful aspect to the army of shoes, enough to suggest what will prove true: she is scared and angry about being left behind while my grandmother was out lunching, teaing, shopping, and disappearing into the desert for weeks at a time. Unable to hold her mother's attention, she spent two years in the care of a baby nurse, then seven years with

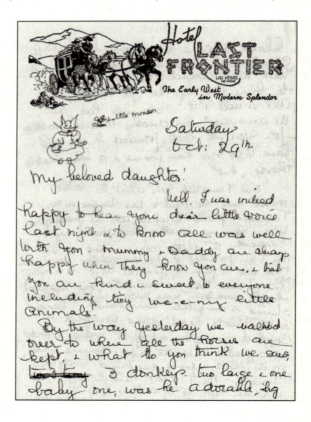

Libby and another seven with Nea, who became one of my godmothers. My mother doesn't fight with Libby or Nea. She goes to them for advice; she tells them things about my father that she doesn't tell me.

That's how I find out he's a preacher—Libby lets it slip. She says he is a "man of God," leaving me with the impression that he left because he is holier than we are.

"YOU DON'T NEED to spend so long on each one," my grandfather says of the birds of prey I am making out of aluminum foil. They don't have to be any shape in particular, he says. "All they have to do is reflect the sun, so it startles the birds." Birds can't hurt citrus fruit or avocados, but they peck through the thin skin of peaches and plums, tearing into them with their beaks.

"It's better if they look like raptors." I am so sure of this, and so stubborn, that he doesn't try to dissuade me, so I go on making them, punching a hole in each, just between where the two wings come out of its back, to thread a string through. They don't look like birds because they are never flying straight, only upside-down or with one wing pointing at the sky, the other at the ground, or tangled up in the string.

Behind the drawn curtains of her bedroom, my mother is missing. I don't remember her leaving, because I didn't see it happen. Like the pretty pie-crust table or the nightstand, she vanishes while I am at school. Or maybe, like one of our Persian carpets, she magics herself into flight and slips out a window and into the sky. However it happens, one afternoon I knock on her door and when there's no answer go into her room and see how many things are missing, see what she cared to take and what she left behind.

I visit the room every day, several times a day if it's a weekend. I avoid the bed's coverlet, as it wrinkles in ways I can never get straight. But I allow myself the rocking chair, as its wood seat can't betray my trespass. The room has its own little fireplace with a hearth of Delft tile, a polished copper hood, and a firebox so clean it looks as if it's never held a fire within. The bed's sheets are changed and the room dusted, as if it expects its occupant's imminent return. Whenever it is, we both know, the bedroom and I, it will not be for as long as a night. She gusts through its door and immediately to the right, into her dressing room, where she flicks through the hangers as though they were on a rack at Saks, ponders the shoes from the height of her hazel eyes, not bothering to bend down. Sometimes she deposits clothes still shrouded in the dry cleaner's plastic bags. Those I examine through the film, as a past mistake proved it unwise to lift the bag off the dress and leave evidence of myself in the form of wrinkles in the white paper shoulders set like a stole over it.

A few times, before she moved out, she woke to find I'd crawled into her bed, and she didn't return me to my room. Instead she let me go on sleeping. Once when I opened my eyes I saw hers regarding me. Young as I am, I know the bad bargain my mother has made. Terrible things happen in life just as in books, where little match girls die in the street, trying to keep warm by lighting what they're meant to sell. As if in a fairy tale, an accident of some kind has delivered me to my mother. Though not a bad child, I am yet one who has befallen my mother, like the red shoes that drove disobedient Karen to chop off her own feet before they danced her to death.

"PLEASE DON'T STOP," I ask my grandfather when I find out why he has traveled only as a passenger in the new car, with my grandmother behind the wheel. "Please, please, please."

I go on asking long after I can tell it's useless. He's not going to change his mind. A decision has been made, out of my hearing or after I've gone to sleep: my grandfather will no longer drive.

"I don't see why." I stand behind him as he kneels down to fill the little set of test tubes with pool water, to check the water's pH, chlorine level, and two other things I never remember. He sets the tubes on the deck and uses a dropper to add a different chemical to each vial. Three of the four go different shades of yellow and orange, and one turns magenta; the sun comes through them like it would come through stained glass and paints the lip of the pool. My grandfather turns the set of test tubes upside-down over the water; the colors disappear. He gets up and dusts off his knees.

"Why can't you just take me to school and that's all? Nana can drive everywhere else."

"No," he says, "especially not you."

"But it wasn't your fault! Everyone says so!" What I don't say is that even if it were, it wouldn't make him a less safe driver than my mother, who now comes every morning to collect me and drop me off at school on her way to work.

As she is always late, she speeds down the driveway and lurches into traffic while pulling curlers from her hair. She drives with one foot on the brake and the other on the accelerator and applies mascara at stoplights. Lipstick is easier because it requires only one hand, so she can do it in the rearview mirror, which is tilted toward her face rather than at the traffic behind her. It's hard to say which is worse, keeping my eyes open or keeping them closed.

If I protest directly to her, she'll use her Gorgon eye to freeze me to my seat—I'll be stuck there forever, whether we have another accident or not. Saying anything to my grandparents can only result in a row that makes my mother like me that much less.

"It's a matter of reflexes," my grandfather says of the accident.

"The brakes failed!"

"But perhaps there was a way to avoid hitting the tree. Maybe I reacted too slowly. That happens when you get—"

"You are not old!" This is the one time in my life that I yell at my grandfather. We are both astonished. "You are not old! You are not! You are not!"

I don't let him console me. I stamp my foot—another first—and run away and up the tree and sit in my chair for as long as I can stand to be alone.

Quintessential Robert Byrd architectural masterpiece set amid lush gardens. Design elements include the whimsical and storybook features you would expect in a Robert Byrd. The large home includes the most inviting, spacious public rooms with trademark ceilings, curves, and built-ins + 2 beds + huge master suite + maids + office upstairs. The ¾ acre lot includes lush landscaping, sparkling pool/ waterfall, cabana, two car garage and huge circular drive to accommodate 12 cars. This is truly a one of a kind property in a prime location not to be missed.

THE FIRST THING I think is not that I've come upon a real estate listing—I have no idea how houses are bought

and sold. But no matter its purpose, I recognize the description as that of Sunset and am concerned that it be faithful. I know we live in a Byrd house, but I always thought the architect's name was spelled Bird, as one whimsical feature is the birdhouses built into the home, like the six, outlined white, under the peaked eaves of my mother's bedroom. My grandfather is proud of the "twelve-inch by twelve-inch circular beam" he points out to company, and our almost empty living room below it is quite large. The breakfast nook and telephone desk are built in. Four bedrooms: my grandparents' big one, my mother's, mine, and Tina's old room. It should say *housekeeper*, as *maid* is impolite. The cabana must be what we call the pool house. But upstairs is not an office, it's always been a library, and I've never seen twelve cars parked in our driveway.

My grandfather calls me outside and I startle and put the paper where I found it, on the built-in telephone desk.

"Come here!" he calls again, and I run to the front door, skirting the potentially lethal doormat to step out the front door and into a snowfall. Flakes spiral lazily down from above.

"It doesn't snow in Los Angeles," I say, and he shrugs.

No matter what the flakes touch—the driveway, the grass, my sweater, his eyeglasses—they vanish. It doesn't occur to me that his smile responds to my mystified delight. I take it as a confession—proof that he's the engineer of this impossibility. The flakes are not of this place but transported by some form of sorcery, a trick of summoning, of bending time to borrow a flurry fifty years old.

I look up to watch them fall from above, try to follow a single flake's trajectory. At last one lies down on my eye's pupil. Like all the others, it has come many years and even more miles to turn at my touch to plain water.

. . .

At bedtime I am still thinking of the flakes, still seeing them. All I want to talk about is snow. I forget about the paper left on the desk, forget to ask my grandfather what purpose the description of our house serves. "Let me think a moment," he says when I ask him to tell me something I don't know about Alaska. "Let me think."

"IT DOESN'T ADD up."

This is the one thing on which my mother, my grandmother, and my grandfather can agree: it does not add up.

"Where does it go?" my grandmother demands. "Tell me. You owe me that much, at least."

My mother shrugs: her mystification is equal to my grandmother's. Again, as it was when my grandfather was sent to the front in the First World War, his jump on figures is no advantage; perhaps it is the opposite. I can tell he's the only one of them offended by the tangle of crumpled bills in my grandmother's hysterically waving hand. One, salvaged from the trash, is torn in half and taped crookedly back together. My mother hijacked it from the mailbox and ripped it up before anyone saw it, but not quite in time. Or so it was made to appear as the wastepaper basket is pulled out from the shadow under the desk, the two halves of the bill laid neatly on top, not so much unconcealed as announced. A little *mise en scène* for my grandmother to come upon.

Because it's not enough to scream at each other in French; my mother and grandmother wage war by means other than direct argument. Their slamming of doors and drawers is not a random display of temper but a language in itself. The silverware drawer produces a shrill clatter, the back door's glass panes rattle; the front door is too heavy to slam properly, so they make do with others.

"Why wouldn't I think so?" My grandmother is still flapping the crumpled sheaf of bills. "What other explanation can there be! It's tens of thousands! Where on God's green earth did it go?"

There it is, the *idée fixe*: there is no blight that cannot be traced back to lesbian interference. What conclusion is my grandmother to draw other than that my mother's roommate is a sponger, and a very successful one? And if my mother really wants to model her life on her aunt's, maybe there's another lesbian, maybe one is not enough. Perhaps an unnamed echo of the Jordan Almond lurks within the apartment that has no address—none my mother will reveal. For what other reason could there be for a person hiding where she lives from her own mother?

Preventing my grandmother from raiding my mother's putative seraglio seems good enough reason to me, but it does leave my mother vulnerable to observations about why an innocent person might be secretive. From across the vast Atlantic, the malignant power of Cecily has stolen my mother away.

Because if it isn't the occult drain of lesbians, then what is it?

The criminal involvement of an unscrupulous trust officer? This is my mother's suggestion. Having made it, she goes back and forth down the hall slamming all the bedroom doors and the bathroom's as well. I stay clear of mine as she approaches, flings it open, and bangs it shut.

My grandmother agrees that there are other forms of larceny than lesbian ones and accuses my mother of pawning the missing jewels, of which I suspect at least a portion are fantastic, things of phantasms, of pipe dreams. And yet George will repeat the same question each time I visit: "Tell me, sweetie pie," he'll say, "what became of the jewels?" using the same word as my grandmother, *jewels* rather than *jewelry*: a different order of adornment, like crown jewels.

"There were rather a lot," Aunt Aziza says. "At least, that was what I understood."

To hear family other than my grandmother speak of them with the same conviction as her own, and with the same hushed and reverent tone reserved for the departed, is to fall prey to their certainty: surely there are jewels, a great number of them, and valuable beyond measure. A pirate's chest of them dredged up from the subterranean markets of Baghdad, the kind whose lid won't close because it's over-filled with rubies fit for a sultan's turban, diamonds the size of ostrich eggs, and sapphires, emeralds, and pearls.

ALONG WITH THE papers my grandmother saves in her mother's lockbox are objects, a few of great value, but not quite great enough. In any case, they have been preserved by a sentiment that will not let them go: her father's pocket watch, solid gold, and her mother's gold Boucheron compact and lipstick case, heavy enough to weigh down an evening bag. And things of purely sentimental value: the announcement of my grandmother's birth in the London *Times,* a sterling silver rattle with an ivory handle, her parents' death certificates, each signed by the coroner in Cap Martin. But not a single jewel, no more than there is in the bank's safe-deposit box.

Whatever's left remains in the possession of Cecily, who dies suddenly, once again proving my grandmother's claim of precognition, as she dreams of a funeral on the eve of her sister's death. Before breakfast I come upon her standing in front of the telephone, watching it as though it were animate, speaking from its cradled receiver.

"What are you doing, Nana?"

But she doesn't answer the question until after dinner,

when she describes her dream as "lugubrious," the funeral "one of those gruesome old-fashioned kinds that no one has anymore. Dirges, paid mourners, and miles of black crepe, and everyone's faces hidden under black veils. Rainy, windy."

All she says in the moment is, "Someone has died." The phone rings within an hour. It is Cecily who died, of a cerebral hemorrhage, as did the sisters' father.

Almost as terrible as the death itself is that it forces my grandmother to get her *papers in order* and acquire a *new passport,* requiring a trip to the bank's safe-deposit box, where lie occult documents capable of deporting a person, or worse.

"What would be worse?" I want to know. But there is no worse whose name she will utter.

Incredibly—*incroyablement*—upon arriving in Nice, accompanied by my mother, my grandmother discovers that Cecily has bequeathed every last jewel to Mlle. Garrigues. The two of them come home with no more than a big manila envelope filled with documents and my mother's stories of my grandmother's travails with escalators, which include the heroism of a tall Parisian who, stepping out of the growing queue of travelers behind my grandmother, frozen before the moving stairs, lifted her by the armpits and set her, shocked into silence, on the first gnashing step to emerge from the slit before her feet.

"Sporting of him," my grandmother says, as if she found a spot of chivalry worth the risk of death by escalator.

Again, absolutely incredible—*absolument incroyable!*— they have barely returned from Europe when Mademoiselle expires and leaves the whole heap of them (the further they are from us, the larger the collection grows) to her brother,

M. Garrigues, who, by virtue of existing, summons rage from my grandmother, a rage separate from our woes about money.

It's not that the missing jewels might save us—nothing ever does, somehow. It's that he has defiled them. That Mademoiselle got them in the first place was an affront from which my grandmother has yet to recover. But this, the brother: it is too much. He is a mountebank, a *voleur,* a *voyou* (a thief, a lout).

"My mother's jewels. To think of it. In the hands of that lout of a brother of that beastly, beastly woman . . ."

A flurry of letters between her attorney in Los Angeles and the one representing M. Garrigues in Nice adds up to the impossibility of contesting this outrage. Incredibly— how can things have taken so extraordinarily bad a turn?— there is nothing to be done. The lout is the rightful owner of the jewels.

Still, where are they, my grandmother's share? Somehow we have lost them, our magical inheritance. For once upon a time we were among the guardians of the fabled pearl-lined cloak, the wealth of the sultanate, so heavy only the greatest of sheiks had the strength to bear its weight with grace. Others before him had toppled, but not David Sassoon.

It swept the ground—it must have; otherwise people would have been able to see the pearls, they would have caught the light, shined, invited discovery. So the cloak swept the ground and the pearls along the hem were muddied— but only in the moment.

My grandmother picks up her pearls from the Limoges dish where she leaves them when she isn't bathing or sleeping.

I ask her why she wears them all the time when my

mother changes necklaces with her clothes, and she says pearls must be worn each day, otherwise they die, their luster disappears. She shows me one she'll have to have removed when the necklace is next restrung, and I see she's right; its color has changed, and the light has evaporated from its surface, the way it does from the eye of something dying, a bird that hit the window.

"But tell me, sweetie pie, really. What became of the jewels?" George insists.

THE JEWELS ARE a romance. The trust is not. The jewels are an idea. The trust is a reality, a shrinking reality. The rococo intricacies and Chinese boxes of my grandmother's trust defy reason. Its principal shrivels, its dividends climb and fall like a game of Chutes and Ladders. There are gaps, there are lacunae, there are inkblots and clots of calculations in pencil too faint to read. Margins and percentages that ought to align don't. Letters to trust officers in New York, asking—pleading—for just a sliver of the principal, enough to spread new blacktop over the cracked driveway or to pay off the astronomical veterinary bills, as my grandmother's hypochondria extends to our cats.

Invasions and sieges and chaotic transfers of debated funds generate mountains of papers that burst the bounds of a banker's box—tax records and correspondence among attorneys, a stupefying number of last testaments and codicils, so many that the older ones have been evicted from the file cabinet and moved upstairs to the library closet. One year my grandmother amends her intentions every other month. Suspected treachery—I know better than to ask what—on the part of a cousin, Cherry, upsets a complex hierarchy reflecting both devotion and duty and leaves her favor shifting from one to another beneficiary, just as people are invited into and out of her address book.

As my fingers are straight where hers are crooked, I copy

it for her when there are too many slashes—death or excom-
munication: they look the same, a bend sinister—and too
many new addresses pinched in the margins. Once a year,
perhaps. It makes me feel grown-up, that she entrusts it all
to me. A new address book arrives from Smythson in London, navy blue, like the trademark Wafer diary; eight inches
high and five inches wide, it sits on the table with the phone,
just across from the breakfast nook. A–H, I–P, Q–Z. I do it
in thirds so my hand doesn't cramp.

"Why would I, when I know you're doing it perfectly?"
she says when I ask if she wants to check to make sure I'm
doing a good job. As with the Blue Chip stamps, she knows
that I am slow and meticulous, that first I write in faint
pencil and then trace over the letters with ink. There's never
a mistake. My grandfather has been checking my homework
for years, so I know better than to make one.

"Honestly, darling," my grandmother says as she pages
through the revised address book with wonderment. "I don't
know how you have the patience."

It isn't patience, though, it's gratification, redemption,
bringing order to chaos.

It's no different from my grandfather's ledgers.

Every cost of Sunset's making, every subsequent repair.
Reinforcing the foundation of the west side of the house;
replacing three water heaters, a rain gutter, and a water-
spout; building a shade house for ferns and herbs and flowers
that don't like the sun; a new front-door lamp: in 1961, the
year of my birth, Sunset demanded almost $15,000, with
insurance included. A single line is written in pencil, no
amount specified, a question asked soon after I arrived: was
it time to refinance the mortgage?

The precise regularity of the numerals, the exact place-

ment of each, columns of figures that descend without stray-
ing from the lines. The numerals slanted toward the right,
like his handwriting. As he never has to erase, he makes his
calculations in ballpoint pen, years' worth without a blot or
wobble.

The fullness of the accounting, its specificity—$49.50
for the door lamp—all the way back to 1944.

In years hence I'll pass my fingers over its pages, feel how
his sure and forthright pen has embossed them like Braille.

Perhaps I shouldn't ask by what means, but for what
purpose am I to strip my spirit from my flesh when it's not
just people and animals and trees but all the world that
speaks to me?

A stone can bleed, a reed can think, a page of my grandfather's ledger joins our two hands across the years. Invites
me, in the dark, to fit mine into his and feel the life left in it.

ASTRONAUT ICE CREAM comes in bags, like potato chips, and Space Food Sticks come in shades of brown. I don't know what either tastes like, and I am unlikely to find out, as I know better than to offer anything from my lunch bag in trade. I don't tell other children what meat it is between slices of baguette—we are a household without loaves of bread, we have only long baguettes, which produce round little sandwiches—not since I told the girl sitting next to me at the lunch table that it was tongue, which I like but no longer eat in public.

"What do you mean, tongue?"

"Just tongue, that's all."

She sticks her own out in response. "Tongue as in tongue?" she says, and then she sticks it out again and wiggles it. The whole table waits for my answer.

"From a cow." I gird myself for the inevitable pantomimes of gagging and retching and clutching at their throats as if poisoned.

Marmite, liverwurst, cream cheese and minced olives: whatever sandwich it is, no one else wants it.

I don't see how anything that travels as slowly as *Apollo 11* can be exciting to watch, yet my grandfather stares at the screen of the big Zenith television as though afraid he'll miss

something if he leaves the room. He sits there for days, watching nothing happen. The spaceship is a white dot in vast darkness, interrupted every so often by a little movie of a rocket coming apart.

"What's a simulation?" The word is written under each movie, like a picture's caption.

"It's a . . . I think in this case it's an animated model."

"It's fake?"

"It's to show you what you can't see from so far away."

"It isn't the real rocket."

"No."

Apollo moves at nearly 25,000 miles per hour—or, my grandfather calculates for me, around 275 times faster than my grandmother on the freeway—and when it at last touches down on the moon's pocked blue surface and the strangely bundled ghost of Neil Armstrong emerges from the capsule, floating on an umbilicus, to make his great step for mankind, my grandfather grabs my arm and shakes me, as though he'd caught me at some mischief, although he has never done that: shaken me in anger. He's given me a potch on my tuchus, but that's not the same; that's just a playful reprimand for my being impertinent or pretending not to hear when Nana calls me to my bath.

"I would have thought they were mad," he says, and gives me another shake. "Mad! Do you understand?"

"Yes," I say, even though I don't. I pull my arm out of his grasp and he turns his attention back to the television.

THE CHECK, WHEN it arrives, is small.

In fact, it is so small that it has already been spent before it is deposited, to cover an overdraft.

"What does that mean?"

"It means we're ruined," my grandmother says, and she retreats to her room without screaming on the other side of the softly closed door.

"Like this," she says a few weeks later, and shows me how to fold the blanket and sheet around the corners at the foot of my bed.

"Like wrapping a present."

"They're called hospital corners."

Every day now, before I leave for school, my room has to be tidy, the bed made perfectly, the spread unwrinkled, teddy bears lined up.

"Why?" I ask my grandfather, who confirms what I fear: Sunset is "on the market."

"What does that mean?" I ask, knowing the answer.

"It means we are moving to a new house."

I nod. I want to run. I want to be in the avocado, up the avocado, but my feet, like my tongue, are stilled.

Instantly, the real estate agent becomes a woman whom I hate with an intensity usually directed at my mother's boyfriends: both agents of loss. She carries a black vinyl folder with "listings" inside. Houses that are listed for sale.

But as the months pass, *listed,* which at first sounded bad, begins to feel like a warning. The idea of it, without a buyer's offer, is one I can ignore.

A few actors look at the house. One mentions the Tate-LaBianca murders, committed less than a mile away when we were in La Jolla two summers ago. That the Manson Family came so close is bad enough, but that Sharon Tate and Roman Polanski's house was also built by Robert Byrd makes it that much worse, as though it were an accessory to murder. I'm not supposed to know about what happened, but everyone does, it's on the front pages of newspapers. The Manson Family wrote on the walls with Sharon Tate's blood.

It is November, it is December, Christmas comes and goes. By the time *listing* turns to *offer* I am so used to hospital corners that I have forgotten what they mean. My reaction to the news that we have lost the house takes everyone, even me, by surprise. For as long as I can, I ignore what anyone says. I make myself deaf to the words.

Every day after school I end up in my grandfather's lap, big girl that I am, ten years old. I don't like it when he reminds me that I am a big girl; it seems like a covert way of saying he's an old man.

The timing of the move is set to coincide with my summer vacation. They take me away before Sunset is dismantled—the remaining furniture, a few antiques among the workaday tables and chests and drawers. My toy box leaves its window seat behind.

ONE THOUSAND AND TWO *Coast Boulevard South. One thousand and two Coast Boulevard South.*

Ten is too old to be quizzed, and La Jolla is so small and safe, its local crime blotter like an empty garage, that I hardly need know our address, but the habit of reciting persists.

One thousand and two Coast Boulevard South—we always rent the same cottage—is not big enough to accommodate my mother and grandmother for more than a weekend at a time, and a weekend is as long as my mother ever stays. After all, she has a *job,* she reminds us all as she bolts on Sunday night, as though it were her weekday labor that afforded us a summer holiday.

The Red Roost.

We take the same cottage every August, a little white clapboard house on the corner of Coast Boulevard South and Ocean Lane, the only one with a big window over the breakfast table, with a hook that pulls from an eye to swing open wide, framing Rocky Point and the ocean beyond it.

"The only one with this exact same view," I say when my grandfather says most cottages have windows. We keep the binoculars between our cereal bowls so we can take turns looking at the fishing boats off the point. The oilcloth under our plates, the plates themselves, the sugar melting under the lid of its bowl: everything is sticky with salt air. When I clear the dishes and take off the cloth, it comes up with a sound like masking tape releasing. Under it, the breakfast table's varnished surface feels tacky, as though it never dried properly. The pillows in what my grandmother calls the day room are heavy, as though filled with wet sand rather than batting, and the wicker chairs, sofa, and chaise beneath them wear so many coats of white paint that their arms, legs, and backs have lost their original outlines. Whoever paints them once a season—it's always freshly white—doesn't dust beforehand but leaves a year's worth of lint and debris caught between the spokes of wicker and settling into its cracks and crevices. Every year the furniture slides that much further out of focus. Melting like the sugar. The telephone table turns like a lazy Susan, and the yellow linoleum on the kitchen floor goes straight up the wall and bends onto the counter. There's a rooster painted on the bread box, a dish drainer in lieu of a washer, and a rag and one year a can of Energine on the back steps for when tar washes up on the beach from an offshore oil derrick's leak. Sand sticks to the adhesive black blobs underfoot, camouflaging them and exiling me from the cottage until I scrape and scrub them off the soles of my feet. By the time my feet are clean, they're also red and smarting.

The quest for the blue chip toaster is suspended for the holiday. Instead my grandmother writes, stamps, and mails what strikes me as a burdensome number of postcards and letters, especially as we are not exploring exotic countries or even new places but tucked into the same place we are every summer, familiar as an old slipper.

"Why are you telling people what we're doing when we always do the same thing?"

No answer. She never does answer while writing a letter, audible conversational interruptions being unworthy of note. To my mother she reports that I am "as brown as a berry," and makes general comments on my health, including my hay fever, how much I slept, and what I ate, as though I were an infant. I feel embarrassed to read them.

I have a summer homework packet, my first ever. As with Latin, I'll discover that I am the sole child to have anticipated it with eagerness rather than dread. Although *The Last of the Mohicans,* by James Fenimore Cooper—I never leave out the author, as he ought to be criminally exposed each time it's mentioned—is the worst and most tedious book I will ever read, I am sure of it. It and the rest of the packet are tucked into one of the compartments in the headboard of my bed, which is like a rolltop desk's, only bigger. One of them is exactly the right size for the Little House books, which I reread in order. I don't let myself skip the ones I don't like, toward the end, when Mary goes blind and Laura grows up and has to marry Alonzo.

There's another compartment for my seashells, sorted into species.

Free to slip out the door at dawn, before my grandparents wake, every morning I run down to the beach before anyone else has first pick of the seashells left by the ebbing tide. As the weeks continue I grow more exacting, sorting them into species, culling out the imperfect ones, using a needle to dig sand out of the pink whorls inside them. Sometimes an undetected hermit crab frees itself from its always temporary home and goes looking for water. In the morning I discover that it crawled a heroic distance before it died, dragging its soft, coiled back end that carried the shell it left behind.

WHEN THE TIDE comes up and the waves lick them back under the water, I move on to the tide pools, catching crabs and minnows with the orange meat from one of the mussels growing on the reef as bait. The only bad part is smashing the mussel's blue shell and digging what's inside out to tie it to a length of dental floss. (It works better than string.) I lower the bait into the middle of a promising-looking pool. Then I wait. It takes a lot of time before the crabs venture out of their holes. Other children stop and watch and wander off when nothing happens, but one girl, so skinny the leg holes of her bathing suit are loose, crouches next to me as I wait for a fiddler crab to approach and close his claw around the swaying scrap of meat. I swipe him up in my net and drop him in my bucket. It's the same with the fish: I catch them when they pause to nibble.

It's a while before the girl tells me her name is Julie. I've almost forgotten she's there when she asks if she can have a turn. She says she has a big brother, a little sister, and a mother she calls Demi. They all live in the Red Roost, a sprawling derelict bungalow notoriously filled with flower children.

"Why did you do that?" she asks when I pour the bucket out into the tide pool, freeing the crabs and fish, which vanish into the cracks. Experience has proved they won't come back out, not within a reasonable wait. Hours later, a scrap of orange meat hangs in the pool untouched.

"If I kept them, they'd die."

"So why catch them?"

"I like seeing what they do when they're trapped in the bucket together." She nods solemnly. The crabs go around and around the bottom of the bucket; the fish dart back and forth above them. It's the same every time, unless I get a big crab, who chases the small ones.

I follow Julie home and step after her through the half-hung front door and into a labyrinth of bead curtains and Chinese folding screens. Block-print Indian bedspreads cover the walls with elephants marching back and forth, and sitar music spins off turntables, more than one of them, all with their arms open wide so there is never a pause in the music, it swarms on and on. Julie's mother says she was named after a little coffee cup, a word, *demitasse,* I cannot separate from the matching lipstick prints of Aunt Cecily and Mlle. Garrigues, often followed by a nasty French limerick my grandmother has retrieved from boarding school: *Mademoiselle Freakadelle, votre chemise n'est pas belle* . . . There's more, but I know better than to say it out loud.

Demi has decorated their two rooms with plants hanging in macramé slings and posters of Janis Joplin and Mahatma Gandhi. She macraméed her own bikini too, so it's a little see-through.

"Do you want to take a shower?" she asks each time I visit. A communal shower has a tiny room of its own, no sink, no toilet, no curtain or tiles, instead a cement floor with a drain. The only light comes from overhead, through the roof. I always say yes. She thinks it's funny that anyone would come home from the beach and want to scrub it off, but she's like everyone else at the Roost. No one cares that I wander in and out of the warren of homes; they don't ask my name.

Julie, her brother, David, and sister, Coco, are three of a floating band of children as feral as the neighbor boys. Critter, St. Bart's (because, his mother says, that's where he was conceived, which I take to mean it is the place where she thought him up), Amy, and Ben-for-Benita: the children who live in the Roost bathe only if they like; no one makes them wash their hair; their skin is either dirty or salty from seawater; their hair is tangled; they dress as they please (in Critter's case, only underpants); they wear flea collars on their ankles. I go back to our cottage with red welts around mine.

"Don't you have another name?" I ask Critter, who shrugs. If he does, no one uses it. There's no one he calls his mother or father. His nose runs green over his top lip, and what he doesn't wipe off with the back of his hand he licks off with his oddly pointed tongue.

"Let her go," my grandfather says when my grandmother protests my running about with children who even from a distance look to have hippies for parents. I am a good girl, he says, and after all, I have no one else to play with. So every day it doesn't rain and we don't go to the Big Beach, as my grandmother calls La Jolla Shores, with its infinite sightseeing potential, or to the San Diego Zoo or horrible sweltering Chula Vista, where one of my grandparents' ancient friends lives, I run faster, wider, farther with the Mini Merry Pranksters, as the Roosters call us. I don't understand the reference, and I don't tell my grandparents what we do all day, which is behave like hooligans.

Demi—they insist on meeting Julie's mother, so she stops by for tea, wearing a plausible sundress—strikes them as impoverished but not unsavory. She promises that we are all supervised, but no one cares if we sneak into hotel pools and climb on roofs to fly kites, or nick a wheeled laundry cart to take turns rolling in it down the hill to the beach. The Roosters think it's funny, and as the Mini Merries are not the neighbor boys, I'm not really disobeying my grandfather when I teach them how to burn up leaves with a magnifying glass.

One afternoon David, who's almost always too old for our company, comes home from surfing with an earache and lies with his head in Demi's lap while she uses an eyedropper to drip heated baby oil into its canal. I watch the clear shining drops fall and she asks me about Christian Science, which she doesn't know is not a polite topic, as it's religion.

"I get it," she says each time I tell her what I have not managed to get.

There are places other than the Red Roost where I am not supposed to go—caves into which a rising tide doesn't flow so much as surge and can trap a person inside—and I go there too. I go to the cliff from which teenage boys wait to dive, and I join the blue-lipped, goose-pimpled line of them, but only when the tide's up, and because I'm too scared to dive, I jump, legs held tight together, toes pointed, arms straight at my sides.

"Thirty feet, maybe thirty-five," my grandfather says when I point it out while we're walking home from the beach. "Why do you want to know?"

"There's boys that jump off it, that's all."

.   .   .

I hear my grandfather call me, and I don't go running but hide where he can't see me, crouched under a neighbor's unkempt rhododendron, barefoot in the sandy dirt, damp and spiderwebby.

I watch until he gives up, goes back in the cottage to tell my grandmother I am nowhere to be seen. Do I know what I'm doing, that I'm running away not to escape his voice but to hear it calling me back? I want to be able to come out from under the rhododendron, but I am frozen there until he gives up. Then I come out, and if there's no one around to play with, I wait for ten minutes, ten minutes at least, before running back to the cottage, banging the screen door as I burst through. Back.

Me in Scripps Park, La Jolla, 1969.

WHEN WE COME home from La Jolla, as always on the Sunday before Labor Day, the new house is not quite ready, so we live for a month in a motel a few miles away.

There's a little kitchen with a tiny refrigerator, sink, and toaster oven to make the frozen dinners we eat at the same table on which I do my homework. It's good there are only the three of us, as the table has only two legs; the side opposite them is stuck to the wall. There are miniature bars of soap that I hoard, not to use but because I like their smallness. I never go anywhere, but they strike me as useful for travel.

It's a full week before the novelty of it wears off and I hate the itchy plaid fabric covering the couch; I think of all the beautiful tartans and how no genuine one could be yellow and brown. There are two twin beds in my grandparents' room. My bed folds out from the itchy plaid couch in the other room. After we fold it back into the couch, we have breakfast in the coffee shop attached to the motel. We've eaten there a few times before I ask my grandparents if I may sit by myself at the counter as if I were grown up enough to eat at restaurants by myself.

There's no harm in it, they agree, and so I sit on the red vinyl seat of a high stool bolted to the floor. Testing it, the idea of being alone in the world. I eat Frosted Flakes out of their own little box; the waitress shows me where one side is perforated and how the wax paper keeps the milk from leaking out. There's a shelf of little boxes behind the counter: Froot Loops, Cocoa Krispies, Cap'n Crunch. I don't really like any of them, and though once it would have seemed impossible, I tire of French toast.

"You belong to those old folks over there?" the waitress asks. I don't need to look to know she's pointing at my grandparents, but I turn around anyway. From a distance, sitting together, without me: those old folks.

"Yes," I say. "They're my grandparents. I live with them."

"Lucky girl. I bet you're spoiled."

"I am," I say, but I don't look back at her. I am staring at them.

Old folks: I have never heard the words without *home* following them.

My grandmother used some of the money from the sale of Sunset, by then heavily mortgaged, to put Libby, ninety, in the best home she could find, which, she admits, is still a terrible place to go. The *haggeries,* my grandmother has always called them.

I try fitting the words on them—*old folks,* like unfamiliar garments—and I think of the man in the kayak, and how a stranger has turned my grandfather's second heart back into a pair of legs.

"WON'T THEY BE angry?" I ask my grandfather when I see all the rocks piled on the driveway of the new house. Pink quartz, purple amethyst. Chalcedony, tourmaline. Obsidian. All broken apart from one another, dulled in places by cement that won't scrape off.

"They were going to tear the pond apart anyway," he says of the new people, so no, they won't be angry he's taken them back.

"All of it? The waterfall and the copper crane? They didn't want any of it?"

My grandfather shows me the crane. Its feet are gray where they had been trapped in cement. My grandfather's shovel, rake, and hoe lie across the top of his wheelbarrow, filled with other tools he hasn't any place to put.

"I'll build a shed," he says, looking at me looking at them.

"Did you bring it? Did you take it out of the tree?" I ask, but already I know he hasn't. It's been left behind.

"I can make another," he says, and I nod.

We both know there isn't a tree to support it. The house, a split-level ranch house on a street called Valley Vista, in Sherman Oaks, *one four two four seven*, sits on a bare hill, nothing between it and the street.

The hill is something called landfill—premade with a little flat top and naked banks channeled by erosion. This

time, to prevent topsoil from running into the gutter, my
grandfather uses English ivy rather than ice plant.

"Why?" I want to know, and he says it grows faster.

At the back of the house, where the hill is steeper, he
ties one end of a rope to a post and runs the other through
his belt loops so he can slowly rappel down the dry incline,
setting sprigs evenly into the dirt. It's my job to stand at the
top and water the newly planted ivy from above, directing
the nozzle of the hose to follow behind his hands.

"Don't tell Nana," he says, and I don't, but I know she
would be right to say he is too old for such tomfoolery. At
the bottom, he shows me where he has dug a single row of
eight holes. He points at each.

"Orange, orange, lemon, lemon, lime, kumquat, plum,
nectarine," he says, naming the future occupants.

"How tall will they be?" He shrugs.

"Maybe about as tall as you are. Dwarf varieties."

In the front of the house, at the end of the driveway, two
incongruous palms stand one on either side of a black metal
mailbox, casting shadows so long they cross the street.

Meanwhile, adjustments are being made to Sunset, each
of which my grandmother announces in a tone of embittered
gratification, as every choice the new owners make is further
confirmation of their poor taste. "They"—they have a name,
the new owners, but it is never mentioned—have torn out
the tile floors and counters from the master bedroom's bath
and replaced them with marble, vulgar enough in itself, but
it seems these Americans will stop at nothing, as the walls
and shower stall are marble as well. Only the ceiling and the
toilet are not marble. They have mistaken the library for an

office; they have replaced the fishpond and vegetable garden with a tennis court.

Indoors, they have, incredibly, painted everything except the floor white, even the walnut paneling in the living room and the bright copper hood over the fireplace in my mother's bedroom. The floor is white, too, but that's carpet, which extends all the way to the front door, covering the foyer's slippery flagstones. Guests will cross the threshold and remain upright. There are white curtains, white furniture, and a white grand piano that my grandmother bets dollars to doughnuts none of them knows how to play.

AT FIRST IT'S hard and then it's easy to imagine Sunset drained of color.

I leave the house as it was the last time I saw it, sparsely furnished, and I cover everything with snow. At night when I close my eyes, I come in the door, chased by a flurry, to discover a blizzard has rushed through the front door and blown out the back, leaving everything furred and sparkling.

Drifts collect in the corners and on the windowsills, lacy fronds of frost trace each pane. Icicles hang from lamp shades and doorknobs and drop like daggers from the mantelpiece. Snow has stilled the clocks' hands and silenced their clamor. The dinner table is set for three, and our beds are turned down, my pajamas left folded under my pillow.

The storm is over, the wind stilled, but flakes spin lazily down, and nothing can stop them. Bit by bit, the outlines of things disappear.

Acknowledgments

My first thanks to my grandparents, who gave me their pasts, and my future.

To my editor, Gerry Howard, who thinks up my books before I do, and to his assistant, the unflappable Nora Grubb.

To Binky, whose support has carried me through sixteen books now. I can't imagine working with another agent.

ILLUSTRATION CREDITS

Unless noted below, images are courtesy of the author

Page 47
© Grove Millican Ltd, United Kingdom
Page 70
Above: Courtesy of The New York Public Library
Page 72
Courtesy of the Virtual Shanghai Project
Page 85
© ullstein bild Dtl./Contributor via Getty Images
Page 123
Public domain via Wikimedia Commons
Page 205
© David Allen Sibley
Page 209
Right: Courtesy of the University of Nevada, Las Vegas,
    Special Collections
Page 250
Public domain via Wikimedia Commons
Page 253
Public domain via Wikimedia Commons

Kathryn Harrison has written the novels *Thicker Than Water,* *Exposure, Poison, The Binding Chair, The Seal Wife, Envy,* and *Enchantments.* Her autobiographical work includes *The Kiss, Seeking Rapture, The Road to Santiago, The Mother Knot,* and *True Crimes.* She has written two biographies, *Saint Thérèse of Lisieux* and *Joan of Arc,* and a book of true crime, *While They Slept.* She lives in Brooklyn with her husband, the novelist Colin Harrison.